Devon R. Blackwell

I0505115

INVESTING MADE EASY

: A Beginner's Guide to Stocks and Bonds

Devon R. Blackwell

Devon R. Blackwell

Devon R. Blackwell

DISCLAIMER

The information provided in this book is for educational purposes only and should not be considered as professional financial advice. Investing involves risks, and readers should consult with a qualified financial professional before making any investment decisions.

Devon R. Blackwell

TABLE OF CONTENTS

Devon R. Blackwell

INTRODUCTION

Why Investing Is Important

Investing helps you grow your wealth over time. By investing your money in assets such as stocks, bonds, or real estate, you can potentially earn a higher return than you would by keeping your money in a savings account.

Investing can help you beat inflation. Inflation is the increase in the price of goods and services over time, and it can erode the purchasing power of your money. Investing can help you keep up with or even exceed the rate of inflation, ensuring that your money retains its value over time.

Investing can help you build a nest egg for retirement. By investing in a diversified portfolio of assets, you can potentially grow your wealth over time and create a retirement fund that will support you in your golden years.

Investing can provide you with passive income. Certain types of investments, such as rental properties or dividend-paying stocks, can provide you with a regular stream of income without requiring you to actively work for it.

Investing can help you achieve your financial goals. Whether you're saving for a down payment on a house, paying off debt, or planning for your children's education, investing can help you reach your financial goals more quickly and efficiently than saving alone.

Investing can help you diversify your income. Relying solely on a single source of income, such as your job, can be risky. By investing in a variety of assets, you can spread out your income streams and reduce your overall risk.

Investing can help you build generational wealth. By investing in assets that appreciate in value over time, you can create a legacy of wealth that can benefit your family for generations to come.

Investing can help you take advantage of compound interest. Compound interest is the process by which your investment earnings generate additional earnings over time. By investing early and consistently, you can harness the power of compound interest to grow your wealth more rapidly.

Investing can help you build financial security. By creating a diversified investment portfolio, you can protect yourself against financial shocks such as job loss, illness, or unexpected expenses.

Investing can be a fulfilling and enjoyable hobby. Many people find investing to be a fascinating and intellectually stimulating pursuit. By learning about different types of assets and investing strategies, you can develop a deeper understanding of the economy and financial markets.

Devon R. Blackwell

How Investing Can Help You Achieve Your Financial Goals

Investing can help you achieve financial freedom. By building a diversified investment portfolio, you can potentially grow your wealth to a level that allows you to retire comfortably and pursue your passions without worrying about money.

Investing can help you pay off debt. By investing your money in assets that generate a higher return than the interest rate on your debt, you can potentially pay off your loans more quickly and efficiently.

Investing can help you save for big-ticket purchases. Whether you're saving for a down payment on a house, a new car, or a dream vacation, investing can help you reach your savings goals more quickly and efficiently than saving alone.

Investing can help you build an emergency fund. By investing a portion of your savings in a low-risk, liquid asset such as a money market account, you can build an emergency fund that will protect you against unexpected expenses or financial shocks.

Investing can help you leave a legacy. By investing in assets that appreciate in value over time, you can create generational wealth that can benefit your family for years to come.

Investing can help you fund your children's education. By investing in a 529 plan or other education savings account, you can save for your children's college education and potentially earn a tax break on your contributions.

Investing can help you achieve your charitable goals. By investing in socially responsible assets or donating a portion of your investment earnings to charity, you can use your wealth to make a positive impact on the world.

Investing can help you achieve financial independence. By building a diversified investment portfolio that generates passive income, you can potentially reach a level of financial independence that allows you to pursue your passions without relying on a traditional job.

Investing can help you build a business. By investing in your own education or in assets that can help you start or grow a business, you can potentially build a successful enterprise that provides financial security and personal fulfillment.

Investing can help you achieve your long-term financial goals. Whether you're saving for retirement, buying a home, or building wealth for the future, investing can help you reach your goals more quickly and efficiently than saving alone.

Investing can help you weather financial storms. By diversifying your investment portfolio across different asset classes, you can potentially reduce your exposure to market volatility and protect yourself against financial shocks.

Investing can help you take advantage of global economic trends. By investing in assets that are poised to benefit from global economic growth, you can potentially earn higher returns than you would by investing solely in your local market.

Investing can help you create a sense of financial security. By building a diversified investment portfolio that generates steady income and grows over time, you can create a sense of financial security that can help you feel more confident about your future.

Investing can help you achieve financial balance. By balancing your investment portfolio across different asset classes and risk levels, you can create a portfolio that aligns with your personal financial goals and risk tolerance.

Investing can help you achieve financial discipline. By developing a consistent investment strategy and sticking to it over time, you can cultivate the habits of discipline and patience that are necessary for long-term financial success.

Investing can help you achieve financial literacy. By learning about different types of assets, investment strategies, and economic trends, you can develop a deeper understanding of the financial world and make more informed investment decisions.

Investing can help you achieve financial self-reliance. By taking control of your finances and building a diversified investment portfolio, you can become less reliant on outside sources of income and more self-sufficient over time.

Investing can help you achieve financial empowerment. By investing in your own education and building wealth over time, you can gain a sense of personal empowerment that can help you achieve your goals and make a positive impact on the world.

Investing can help you achieve financial flexibility. By building a diversified investment portfolio that generates passive income, you can potentially create the freedom and flexibility to pursue your passions and take advantage of new opportunities as they arise.

Investing can help you achieve financial prosperity. By investing in assets that appreciate in value over time, generating passive income, and building wealth over time, you can potentially achieve a level of financial prosperity that allows you to live the life you've always dreamed of.

CHAPTER 1: WHAT IS INVESTING?

Defining Key Terms and Concepts

Investing: Investing is the act of putting money into an asset with the expectation of generating a profit or income from the investment over time.

Asset: An asset is any resource that has value and can be owned. Examples of assets include stocks, bonds, real estate, and commodities.

Risk: Risk is the potential for loss or damage that may occur when investing in an asset. It is important to understand the risks associated with different types of investments and to have a plan in place to manage those risks.

Return: Return is the profit or income generated from an investment over time. This can come in the form of capital gains, dividends, or interest payments.

Portfolio: A portfolio is a collection of investments owned by an individual or organization. A well-diversified portfolio can help manage risk and maximize returns.

Liquidity: Liquidity refers to the ease with which an investment can be bought or sold. Highly liquid investments are those that can be bought or sold quickly and easily, such as stocks and bonds.

Inflation: Inflation is the rate at which the general level of prices for goods and services is rising. It is important to take inflation into account when making investment decisions, as it can erode the purchasing power of your returns over time.

Asset allocation: Asset allocation is the process of dividing your investments among different types of assets, such as stocks, bonds, and real estate. This can help manage risk and optimize returns.

Diversification: Diversification is the practice of spreading your investments across a variety of different assets and sectors. This can help reduce risk and increase the stability of your portfolio.

Stock market: The stock market is a marketplace where shares of publicly traded companies are bought and sold. It is an important indicator of the overall health of the economy and can be a major driver of investment returns.

Devon R. Blackwell

Understanding the Basics of Stocks and Bonds

Stocks: Stocks, also known as equities, represent ownership in a publicly traded company. When you buy a stock, you become a shareholder and are entitled to a portion of the company's profits.

Dividends: Dividends are payments made by a company to its shareholders out of its profits. Not all companies pay dividends, but those that do can provide a reliable source of income for investors.

Price-to-earnings ratio: The price-to-earnings ratio, or P/E ratio, is a measure of a company's valuation. It is calculated by dividing the stock price by the company's earnings per share. A high P/E ratio can indicate that a company is overvalued, while a low P/E ratio can indicate that it is undervalued.

Bonds: Bonds are debt securities issued by governments and corporations to raise capital. When you buy a bond, you are effectively lending money to the issuer and are entitled to regular interest payments and the return of your principal investment when the bond matures.

Coupon rate: The coupon rate is the interest rate paid on a bond. It is typically expressed as a percentage of the bond's face value and is paid out to bondholders at regular intervals.

Yield: The yield is the total return earned on an investment, expressed as a percentage of the original investment. For bonds, the yield is typically calculated by adding the interest payments and any capital gains or losses to the face value of the bond and dividing by the purchase price.

Credit rating: A credit rating is a measure of a company's or government's creditworthiness. It is assigned by credit rating agencies and can have a significant impact on the interest rates that they must pay to borrow money through the issuance of bonds.

Treasury bonds: Treasury bonds are bonds issued by the U.S. government to finance its operations. They are considered one of the safest investments in the world and are often used as a benchmark for other types of bonds.

Corporate bonds: Corporate bonds are bonds issued by companies to raise capital. They typically offer higher yields than government bonds, but are also riskier.

Junk bonds: Junk bonds are bonds issued by companies with lower credit ratings. They typically offer higher yields than other types of bonds to compensate for the additional risk.

Mutual funds: Mutual funds are investment vehicles that pool money from multiple investors to buy a diversified portfolio of stocks, bonds, and other assets. They are a popular way for individual investors to gain exposure to a wide range of investments with relatively low fees.

Index funds: Index funds are a type of mutual fund that tracks a specific market index, such as the S&P 500. They are designed to provide broad market exposure with low fees and are a popular choice for investors who want to minimize their investment costs.

Exchange-traded funds (ETFs): ETFs are similar to mutual funds in that they provide diversified exposure to a portfolio of assets. However, they are traded on stock exchanges like individual stocks and can be bought and sold throughout the trading day.

Active vs. passive investing: Active investing involves trying to beat the market by selecting individual stocks or actively managing a portfolio of investments. Passive investing, on the other hand, involves investing in index funds or ETFs that track the performance of a market index.

Buy and hold strategy: A buy and hold strategy involves buying a diversified portfolio of investments and holding them for the long term, regardless of short-term market fluctuations. This strategy is often used by investors who are focused on long-term growth and income generation.

Dollar-cost averaging: Dollar-cost averaging involves investing a fixed amount of money at regular intervals, regardless of market conditions. This can help reduce the impact of market volatility on your investment returns.

Rebalancing: Rebalancing involves adjusting your investment portfolio periodically to maintain your desired asset allocation. This can help ensure that your portfolio is appropriately diversified and aligned with your investment goals.

Active management vs. passive management: Active management involves trying to outperform the market by actively buying and selling individual stocks or making other investment decisions. Passive management involves simply investing in a diversified portfolio of assets with the goal of matching the performance of a market index.

Systematic risk vs. unsystematic risk: Systematic risk is the risk that is inherent in the overall market or economy, while unsystematic risk is the risk that is specific to a particular company or industry. It is important to understand both types of risk when making investment decisions.

Long-term vs. short-term investing: Long-term investing involves holding investments for several years or even decades with the goal of achieving long-term growth and income generation. Short-term investing, on the other hand, involves buying and selling investments over a shorter period of time with the goal of realizing quick profits. It is important to determine which approach is best suited to your investment goals and risk tolerance.

CHAPTER 2: STOCKS 101

How Stocks Work:

Stocks represent ownership in a company. When you buy a stock, you become a shareholder in that company and have a claim on a portion of its assets and earnings.

Stocks are bought and sold on stock exchanges, which are marketplaces where buyers and sellers can trade shares of publicly traded companies.

The price of a stock is determined by supply and demand. If there are more buyers than sellers, the price of the stock will go up. If there are more sellers than buyers, the price will go down.

The value of a stock can fluctuate based on a variety of factors, including the company's financial performance, market trends, and global events.

Investing in stocks carries risks, including the possibility of losing your entire investment. However, over the long-term, stocks have historically provided higher returns than other types of investments.

Investors can choose to invest in individual stocks or through mutual funds or exchange-traded funds (ETFs), which provide diversification and can help reduce risk.

Successful stock investing requires research, analysis, and patience. It's important to understand the fundamentals of the company and industry you're investing in, as well as to have a long-term investment horizon.

Stock prices are also affected by factors such as dividends, earnings, and price-to-earnings ratios. Understanding these metrics can help investors make more informed decisions about which stocks to buy and when to sell.

It's important to have a well-diversified portfolio when investing in stocks to help mitigate risk. This means investing in a variety of companies across different industries and sectors.

While stock investing can be volatile in the short-term, it can provide significant growth and wealth-building opportunities over the long-term.

How to Buy and Sell Stocks

Buying and selling stocks can be a profitable way to invest your money, but it can also be risky if you don't know what you're doing. Here are some tips that will guide you through the process of buying and selling stocks.

Before you start buying and selling stocks, it's important to understand the risks involved. Stocks can be volatile, and there's always a chance that you could lose money.

The first step in buying and selling stocks is to open a brokerage account. This will give you access to the stock market and allow you to buy and sell stocks.

When choosing a brokerage account, consider the fees they charge for trades, as well as any additional services they offer, such as research tools or investment advice.

Once you have a brokerage account, you'll need to fund it. This can be done by transferring money from your bank account or by depositing a check.

Before you start buying stocks, it's important to do your research. Look at the company's financial statements, read news articles about the company, and research the industry in which the company operates.

When buying stocks, you'll need to decide how many shares you want to buy and at what price. This will depend on your budget and your investment goals.

When selling stocks, you'll need to decide at what price you want to sell. This will depend on the current market price and your investment goals.

When buying and selling stocks, it's important to keep an eye on the stock market. You can use online tools and apps to track stock prices and stay up-to-date on market trends.

One strategy for buying and selling stocks is to diversify your portfolio. This means investing in a variety of stocks in different industries to reduce your risk.

Another strategy for buying and selling stocks is to focus on long-term investments. This means buying stocks that you believe will grow in value over time and holding onto them for years.

When buying and selling stocks, it's important to have a plan. Set specific goals for your investments, and stick to your plan even when the market is volatile.

When buying and selling stocks, it's important to be patient. Stocks can take time to grow in value, so don't expect to get rich overnight.

When buying and selling stocks, it's important to be disciplined. Stick to your investment plan, and don't let emotions cloud your judgement.

One way to minimize risk when buying and selling stocks is to use stop-loss orders. These orders automatically sell your stocks if their value drops below a certain price, limiting your losses.

When buying and selling stocks, it's important to stay informed about the companies you're investing in. Read financial reports, attend shareholder meetings, and keep up with industry news.

When buying and selling stocks, it's important to understand the difference between market orders and limit orders. Market orders buy or sell stocks at the current market price, while limit orders buy or sell stocks at a specific price.

When buying and selling stocks, it's important to understand the concept of bid and ask prices. The bid price is the highest price buyers are willing to pay for a stock, while the ask price is the lowest price sellers are willing to accept.

When buying and selling stocks, it's important to understand the concept of spreads. The spread is the difference between the bid and ask prices, and it represents the cost of buying and selling stocks.

When buying and selling stocks, it's important to understand the concept of commissions. Commissions are fees charged by brokers for buying and selling stocks, and they can add up quickly if you're not careful.

When buying and selling stocks, it's important to understand the concept of dividends. Dividends are payments made by some companies to their shareholders, and they can provide a steady source of income.

When buying and selling stocks, it's important to understand the concept of earnings per share (EPS). EPS is a company's net earnings divided by the number of outstanding shares, and it can be a useful metric for evaluating a company's profitability.

When buying and selling stocks, it's important to understand the concept of price-to-earnings (P/E) ratios. The P/E ratio is a company's stock price divided by its EPS, and it can be a useful metric for evaluating a company's valuation.

When buying and selling stocks, it's important to understand the concept of market capitalization (market cap). Market cap is a company's stock price multiplied by the number of outstanding shares, and it can be a useful metric for evaluating a company's size.

When buying and selling stocks, it's important to understand the concept of technical analysis. Technical analysis involves using charts and other tools to analyze stock price trends and make investment decisions.

When buying and selling stocks, it's important to understand the concept of fundamental analysis. Fundamental analysis involves analyzing a company's financial statements, industry trends, and other factors to make investment decisions.

When buying and selling stocks, it's important to understand the concept of risk management. This involves assessing your risk tolerance and diversifying your portfolio to minimize your risk.

When buying and selling stocks, it's important to understand the concept of market cycles. The stock market goes through cycles of growth and contraction, and understanding these cycles can help you make better investment decisions.

When buying and selling stocks, it's important to understand the concept of market timing. Market timing involves trying to predict when the market will go up or down, and it can be a risky strategy.

When buying and selling stocks, it's important to have a long-term perspective. The stock market can be volatile in the short-term, but over the long-term, it tends to grow in value.

When buying and selling stocks, it's important to remember that there are no guarantees. Investing in the stock market involves risk, and there's always a chance that you could lose money. However, by doing your research, diversifying your portfolio, and sticking to your investment plan, you can increase your chances of success.

How Stocks Work

Stocks are ownership shares in a publicly traded company. When you purchase a stock, you become a shareholder in the company, which means you have a stake in its success or failure.

The value of a stock is determined by the demand for it in the market. If more people want to buy a particular stock, its price will go up, and if fewer people want to buy it, its price will go down.

Stocks are traded on stock exchanges, which are marketplaces where buyers and sellers come together to buy and sell shares in publicly traded companies.

The most common way to buy stocks is through a brokerage account. You can open a brokerage account with a brokerage firm and use it to purchase and sell stocks.

Stocks can be classified into different types based on their size, market capitalization, sector, and other factors. Common stock is the most basic type of stock, and it represents ownership in a company.

Stock prices can be affected by a variety of factors, including economic conditions, company performance, and investor sentiment.

One way to make money with stocks is through dividends. Dividends are payments made by a company to its shareholders, usually in cash, and are typically paid out on a quarterly basis.

Another way to make money with stocks is through capital gains. Capital gains occur when you sell a stock for more than you paid for it.

Buying and holding stocks for the long term is a popular investment strategy, known as buy and hold investing. This strategy involves buying stocks and holding them for an extended period, typically several years or more.

One of the risks associated with investing in stocks is the possibility of losing money. If the value of a stock goes down, you could lose money if you sell it.

Another risk associated with investing in stocks is the possibility of market volatility. Stock prices can be affected by a variety of factors, including economic conditions, company performance, and investor sentiment, which can cause prices to fluctuate wildly.

One way to mitigate the risks associated with investing in stocks is through diversification. Diversification involves investing in a variety of different stocks to spread your risk across multiple companies and sectors.

Another way to mitigate the risks associated with investing in stocks is through dollar-cost averaging. This strategy involves investing a fixed amount of money into a stock or a group of stocks on a regular basis, regardless of the market conditions.

When you buy a stock, you become a part-owner of the company, and you have certain rights as a shareholder, including the right to vote on important company decisions.

Stock prices are often influenced by news events, such as changes in interest rates, economic reports, and company earnings announcements.

The stock market can be affected by a variety of external factors, including geopolitical events, natural disasters, and changes in government policies.

Some investors use technical analysis to predict future stock prices based on past market data, while others use fundamental analysis to analyze a company's financial performance and future growth prospects.

Stock prices can be affected by supply and demand, as well as by the overall state of the economy. When the economy is growing, stock prices tend to rise, and when the economy is in a recession, stock prices tend to fall.

In addition to buying individual stocks, investors can also buy shares in mutual funds or exchange-traded funds (ETFs), which provide exposure to a diversified portfolio of stocks.

Mutual funds are managed by professional fund managers, who make investment decisions on behalf of the fund's investors. ETFs, on the other hand, are passively managed and track a particular index.

The stock market is often used as a barometer of the overall health of the economy, and many economists and policymakers closely monitor stock market trends to gauge economic conditions.

The price of a stock is not always a reflection of the underlying value of the company. Sometimes, stocks can become overvalued or undervalued, based on investor sentiment or market conditions.

Some investors engage in trading strategies, such as day trading or swing trading, which involve buying and selling stocks quickly to capitalize on short-term price movements.

Trading stocks can be risky and requires a significant amount of knowledge and experience. Many novice investors may be better off sticking to long-term investing strategies.

When investing in stocks, it is important to consider your investment goals, risk tolerance, and investment time horizon.

Stocks can provide significant long-term returns, but they are not a guaranteed investment, and past performance is not indicative of future results.

The stock market can be unpredictable and volatile, and investors should be prepared to withstand periods of market downturns.

Successful stock investing requires a disciplined approach, sound investment principles, and a long-term perspective.

Overall, stocks can be an attractive investment option for those seeking long-term growth and capital appreciation. However, it is important to do your research, understand the risks involved, and invest with a disciplined approach.

Whether you are a seasoned investor or just getting started, the stock market can be a complex and challenging environment. By understanding the basics of how stocks work and implementing sound investment principles, you can increase your chances of success and achieve your investment goals over time.

Types of Stocks and Their Risks

There are several different types of stocks, each with their own level of risk and potential for reward. Here are the various types of stocks and the risks associated with each.

Blue-chip stocks: These are shares of companies that have a long history of stable earnings and a strong reputation. They are often seen as safe investments, but there is still a risk of market fluctuations and changes in the industry.

Growth stocks: These are shares of companies that are expected to grow at a faster rate than the market average. They typically reinvest their earnings into the business, rather than paying dividends. These stocks can be more volatile, with the potential for large gains or losses.

Value stocks: These are shares of companies that are undervalued by the market. They may have lower price-to-earnings ratios or higher dividend yields than other companies in the same industry. Investing in these stocks can be a good way to find bargains, but there is a risk that the company may not be able to improve its performance.

Small-cap stocks: These are shares of companies with a small market capitalization, usually under $2 billion. They can be riskier than larger companies, as they may have less financial stability and less established track records.

Mid-cap stocks: These are shares of companies with a market capitalization between $2 billion and $10 billion. They offer a balance between the potential for growth and the stability of larger companies.

Large-cap stocks: These are shares of companies with a market capitalization over $10 billion. They are often seen as stable investments, but may have less potential for growth than smaller companies.

Penny stocks: These are shares of companies that trade for less than $5 per share. They can be very risky, as they may be in early stages of development or have other issues that make them less attractive to investors.

Preferred stocks: These are shares of companies that pay a fixed dividend, similar to a bond. They are less volatile than common stocks, but may have lower potential for growth.

Foreign stocks: These are shares of companies based outside of the investor's home country. They can offer diversification and the potential for high returns, but also carry currency and political risks.

Emerging market stocks: These are shares of companies based in developing countries. They can offer high returns, but also carry higher risk due to political instability and economic volatility.

Defensive stocks: These are shares of companies that are less affected by changes in the economy or market cycles. They may include companies in industries such as utilities, healthcare, or consumer staples.

Cyclical stocks: These are shares of companies that are more affected by changes in the economy or market cycles. They may include companies in industries such as construction, automotive, or technology.

Dividend stocks: These are shares of companies that pay regular dividends to investors. They can provide a steady stream of income, but may have less potential for growth than other types of stocks.

High-yield dividend stocks: These are shares of companies that pay higher-than-average dividends. They can be attractive to income investors, but may be riskier than other dividend stocks.

Growth and income stocks: These are shares of companies that offer both growth potential and dividends. They may be a good choice for investors who want a balance of income and growth.

Blue-chip dividend stocks: These are shares of large, established companies that pay regular dividends. They are often seen as safe investments, but may have lower potential for growth.

Technology stocks: These are shares of companies in the technology industry. They can offer high growth potential, but can also be more volatile and subject to rapid changes in technology and consumer preferences.

Energy stocks: These are shares of companies in the energy sector, such as oil and gas companies. They can be affected by fluctuations in commodity prices and changes in government regulations.

Healthcare stocks: These are shares of companies in the healthcare industry, such as pharmaceutical and biotechnology companies. They can be affected by regulatory changes, clinical trial results, and patent expirations.

Consumer goods stocks: These are shares of companies that produce consumer goods, such as clothing, food, and household products. They can be affected by changes in consumer trends and economic conditions.

Financial stocks: These are shares of companies in the financial sector, such as banks and insurance companies. They can be affected by changes in interest rates, economic conditions, and regulatory changes.

Real estate stocks: These are shares of companies that own or manage real estate properties, such as office buildings, shopping centers, and apartments. They can be affected by changes in property values and rental rates.

Industrial stocks: These are shares of companies in the industrial sector, such as manufacturing and construction companies. They can be affected by changes in demand for their products and services, as well as economic conditions.

Defensive sector stocks: These are shares of companies in industries that tend to perform well during economic downturns, such as utilities, healthcare, and consumer staples. They may be less volatile than other types of stocks, but may also have less potential for growth.

Emerging market sector stocks: These are shares of companies in developing countries, in industries such as technology, energy, and consumer goods. They can offer high potential for growth, but may also be more volatile and subject to political and economic risks.

Low-volatility stocks: These are shares of companies that tend to experience smaller price fluctuations than the broader market. They can be attractive to investors who want to minimize risk, but may also have lower potential for growth.

High-beta stocks: These are shares of companies that tend to experience larger price fluctuations than the broader market. They can be attractive to investors who are willing to take on more risk in exchange for the potential for higher returns.

Cyclical sector stocks: These are shares of companies in industries that are sensitive to changes in the economy, such as construction, automotive, and technology. They can be more volatile than other types of stocks, but may also offer higher potential for growth.

Defensive stock funds: These are mutual funds or exchange-traded funds (ETFs) that invest in defensive sector stocks, such as utilities, healthcare, and consumer staples. They can offer diversification and stability to a portfolio.

Growth stock funds: These are mutual funds or ETFs that invest in growth stocks, such as technology and healthcare companies. They can offer the potential for high returns, but may also be more volatile than other types of funds.

In conclusion, there are various types of stocks with different levels of risks and potential rewards. It is important for investors to understand these differences and to consider their investment goals, risk tolerance, and time horizon when selecting stocks or stock funds. While some stocks may offer high potential for growth, they may also come with higher levels of risk. On the other hand, defensive stocks or funds may offer more stability but may have lower potential for growth. Ultimately, a well-diversified portfolio that includes a mix of different types of stocks and funds can help investors manage their risk and achieve their investment objectives.

What Is a Stock Market Index?

A stock market index is a benchmark that tracks the performance of a group of stocks. It provides a snapshot of the overall performance of a particular market or sector. Some popular stock market indices include the S&P 500, the Dow Jones Industrial Average, and the NASDAQ Composite. Investors can use stock market indices to compare the performance of their own investments to the broader market or to identify trends in specific industries or sectors.

What Is a Stock Split?

A stock split is a corporate action in which a company divides its existing shares into multiple shares. For example, a 2-for-1 stock split would result in an investor receiving two shares for every one share they previously owned. The value of the stock doesn't change, but the number of shares outstanding increases. Stock splits are often done to make the stock more affordable for individual investors or to increase liquidity in the market.

What Is a Dividend?

A dividend is a distribution of a portion of a company's earnings to its shareholders. Dividends are typically paid in cash but can also be paid in the form of additional shares of stock or other assets. Companies that pay dividends tend to be more established and stable, and dividends can provide a steady source of income for investors.

What Is a Blue-Chip Stock?

A blue-chip stock is a stock of a company that has a long history of stable earnings and is considered to be a leader in its industry. Blue-chip stocks are typically large-cap stocks and are considered to be less risky than smaller, less established companies. Some examples of blue-chip stocks include Apple, Microsoft, and Johnson & Johnson.

What Is a Growth Stock?

A growth stock is a stock of a company that is expected to grow at a faster rate than the overall market. These companies typically reinvest their earnings back into the business to fuel growth, rather than paying dividends. Growth stocks can be more volatile than other types of stocks because their success is often tied to the success of the company's growth prospects.

What Is a Value Stock?

A value stock is a stock of a company that is considered to be undervalued by the market. These companies may have low price-to-earnings ratios or other factors that make them appear to be trading at a discount. Value stocks can provide a good opportunity for investors looking for long-term growth potential.

What Is a Penny Stock?

A penny stock is a stock of a company that trades for less than $5 per share. These stocks are often associated with small, newly established companies and can be highly volatile. Investors should exercise caution when investing in penny stocks, as they can be more susceptible to fraud and manipulation.

What Is a Stock Exchange?

A stock exchange is a marketplace where stocks are bought and sold. The most well-known stock exchange in the United States is the New York Stock Exchange (NYSE), but there are several other exchanges, including the NASDAQ and the Chicago Stock Exchange. Stock exchanges provide a centralized location for buyers and sellers to trade stocks and help to facilitate the smooth functioning of the stock market.

What Is Market Volatility?

Market volatility refers to the tendency of the stock market to experience frequent and sometimes significant fluctuations in value. Market volatility can be caused by a variety of factors, including changes in economic conditions, political events, and investor sentiment. Investors should be prepared for market volatility and have a long-term investment strategy in place to help them weather periods of market turbulence.

Brokers can work for a brokerage firm or operate independently. When choosing a broker, investors should consider factors such as fees, services offered, and the broker's reputation.

What Is a Stock Portfolio?

A stock portfolio is a collection of stocks owned by an investor. Investors can build a portfolio that is diversified across different sectors and types of stocks to help manage risk and maximize potential returns. A well-diversified portfolio should include a mix of large-cap, mid-cap, and small-cap stocks, as well as growth and value stocks.

What Is Stock Market Index?

A stock market index is a benchmark used to measure the performance of a group of stocks. The most well-known stock market index in the United States is the Dow Jones Industrial Average (DJIA), which is made up of 30 large-cap stocks. Other popular indices include the S&P 500 and the NASDAQ Composite. Investors can use indices to track the performance of the stock market as a whole or to compare the performance of their own stock portfolio to the broader market.

What Is Stock Market Trading?

Stock market trading is the buying and selling of stocks on a stock exchange. Investors can trade stocks through a brokerage account, either online or with the assistance of a broker. Trading stocks can be a profitable endeavor, but it is important for investors to have a solid understanding of market trends, stock valuation, and risk management strategies.

What Is a Stock Market Bubble?

A stock market bubble occurs when the prices of stocks become significantly overvalued relative to their underlying fundamentals. This can happen when investor sentiment becomes overly optimistic and leads to a buying frenzy. Eventually, the bubble bursts, causing stock prices to plummet and leaving many investors with significant losses. It is important for investors to be aware of market trends and to exercise caution when investing during periods of market exuberance.

What Is Stock Market Regulation?

Stock market regulation refers to the laws and regulations that govern the operation of the stock market. In the United States, stock market regulation is overseen by the Securities and Exchange Commission (SEC), which is responsible for ensuring that companies and brokers comply with federal securities laws. Stock market regulation helps to protect investors and maintain the integrity of the stock market.

What Is Stock Market Analysis?

Stock market analysis is the process of evaluating the performance of individual stocks or the stock market as a whole. This can involve analyzing financial statements, market trends, and economic indicators to determine the potential for future growth or decline. Investors can use stock market analysis to inform their investment decisions and to help manage risk.

What Is Stock Market Forecasting?

Stock market forecasting is the process of using data and statistical models to predict future stock market performance. This can involve analyzing historical data, economic indicators, and other factors to develop a forecast of market trends. While stock market forecasting can be a useful tool for investors, it is important to remember that past performance does not guarantee future results and that stock market forecasting can be subject to significant error.

Chapter 3: Bonds 101

Bonds are a type of debt security issued by companies, municipalities, and governments to raise capital. Essentially, a bond is an IOU that promises to repay the investor their original investment plus interest on a specified date in the future.

When an entity issues a bond, they are borrowing money from investors. In return, the investor receives a promise of repayment and regular interest payments over the life of the bond.

The interest rate on a bond, also known as the coupon rate, is set at the time the bond is issued. This rate remains fixed for the life of the bond and determines the amount of interest paid to the investor.

Bonds can have different maturities, ranging from a few months to several decades. The longer the maturity, the higher the interest rate typically is, to compensate the investor for the risk of inflation and changes in interest rates.

Bonds are typically traded in the bond market, where they are bought and sold by investors. The market value of a bond can fluctuate based on changes in interest rates and the financial health of the issuer.

When a bond reaches its maturity date, the issuer is obligated to repay the principal amount of the bond to the investor, in addition to the final interest payment.

Bonds are considered less risky than stocks, as they offer a fixed return and are backed by the issuer's ability to repay the debt. However, there is still some risk involved, particularly if the issuer defaults on their debt obligations.

There are several different types of bonds, including corporate bonds, municipal bonds, and government bonds. Each type has its own characteristics and risks.

Corporate bonds are issued by corporations and typically offer higher interest rates than government bonds, but are considered riskier due to the potential for default.

Municipal bonds are issued by local governments to finance public projects, such as schools and highways. They are generally considered to be less risky than corporate bonds, but may have lower interest rates.

Government bonds are issued by national governments and are considered to be the safest type of bond, as they are backed by the full faith and credit of the government.

Bond ratings are provided by credit rating agencies and assess the creditworthiness of bond issuers. A high rating indicates a lower risk of default, while a low rating indicates a higher risk of default.

Bond prices are inversely related to interest rates; when interest rates rise, bond prices fall, and vice versa. This is because the fixed interest rate on a bond becomes less attractive when interest rates rise, and investors may demand a higher rate of return to compensate for the increased risk.
Bond prices are also affected by changes in market conditions and the financial health of the issuer. If an issuer's credit rating is downgraded, for example, the market value of their bonds may decline.

Bonds can be purchased individually or through mutual funds or exchange-traded funds (ETFs).

Investing in a bond fund can provide diversification and professional management of the bond portfolio.

Investors can also use bond laddering, a strategy where they purchase bonds with staggered maturities, to balance risk and return in their bond investments.

Inflation risk is a concern for bond investors, as rising inflation can erode the value of the fixed interest payments received from the bond.

Interest rate risk is another factor to consider when investing in bonds. When interest rates rise, the market value of existing bonds falls, and investors may experience a loss if they sell their bonds before maturity.

Callable bonds are another type of bond that can increase the risk for investors. These bonds give the issuer the right to "call" or redeem the bonds before their maturity date, which can leave investors with a lower return if interest rates have fallen since the bond was issued.

Overall, bonds can be an important component of a well-diversified investment portfolio. They offer a fixed income stream, a range of maturities, and varying levels of risk and return. However, it's important for investors to understand the risks involved, particularly the impact of changes in interest rates and inflation, and to choose their bond investments carefully based on their individual goals and risk tolerance.

Types of Bonds and Their Risks

Treasury bonds: These bonds are issued by the US government and are considered to be the safest type of bond because they are backed by the full faith and credit of the government. However, their returns are generally lower than other types of bonds.

Municipal bonds: These bonds are issued by state and local governments to finance public projects such as schools and highways. They are generally exempt from federal taxes and may also be exempt from state and local taxes, making them an attractive option for investors seeking tax-free income.

Corporate bonds: These bonds are issued by corporations to raise money for expansion or other projects. They are generally considered riskier than government bonds because the company could default on its debt if it experiences financial difficulties.

High-yield bonds: Also known as "junk bonds," these bonds are issued by companies with lower credit ratings and are considered to be the riskiest type of bond. They offer higher returns to compensate investors for the increased risk.

Convertible bonds: These bonds allow investors to convert their bonds into shares of the issuing company's stock at a predetermined price. They offer the potential for higher returns if the company's stock price increases but also come with the risk of the company's stock price decreasing.

Callable bonds: These bonds can be redeemed by the issuer before they reach maturity, which can be beneficial for the issuer but may result in lower returns for the investor.

Zero-coupon bonds: These bonds do not pay interest but are sold at a discount to their face value and then redeemed for their full value at maturity. They offer the potential for higher returns but also come with the risk of inflation reducing the value of the investment over time.

Inflation-linked bonds: These bonds are designed to protect investors from the effects of inflation by adjusting their interest payments and/or principal value to account for changes in inflation.

Floating-rate bonds: These bonds have variable interest rates that adjust periodically based on changes in an underlying benchmark interest rate. They offer protection against rising interest rates but also come with the risk of declining interest rates reducing returns.

Foreign bonds: These bonds are issued by foreign governments or companies and are subject to the risks of currency exchange rates and political instability in the issuing country.

Mortgage-backed securities: These securities are created by pooling together a group of mortgages and then selling bonds backed by the mortgage payments. They offer the potential for higher returns but also come with the risk of default if a large number of borrowers stop making their mortgage payments.

Asset-backed securities: These securities are backed by pools of assets such as car loans or credit card debt. They offer the potential for higher returns but also come with the risk of default if borrowers stop making their payments.

Collateralized debt obligations (CDOs): These securities are created by pooling together a group of other securities, such as mortgage-backed securities or asset-backed securities, and then selling bonds backed by the income generated from the underlying securities. They were a major contributor to the 2008 financial crisis and are generally considered to be very risky.

Sovereign bonds: These bonds are issued by foreign governments and are subject to the risks of political instability, currency exchange rates, and other economic factors in the issuing country.

Subordinated bonds: These bonds are lower in priority than other types of bonds issued by the same company or government, meaning that they are at greater risk of not being repaid in the event of default.

Perpetual bonds: These bonds have no maturity date and pay interest indefinitely. They offer the potential for steady income but also come with the risk of inflation reducing the value of the investment over time.

Structured notes: These bonds are created by combining a traditional bond with a derivative instrument, such as an option or a swap. They offer the potential for higher returns but also come with the risk of the derivative instrument not performing as expected.

Senior secured bonds: These bonds are backed by specific assets of the issuing company or government, making them less risky than other types of bonds issued by the same entity.

Senior unsecured bonds: These bonds are not backed by specific assets of the issuing company or government, making them riskier than senior secured bonds.

Perpetual subordinated bonds: These bonds have no maturity date and are lower in priority than other types of bonds issued by the same company or government, making them very risky.

Samurai bonds: These bonds are issued in Japan by foreign entities and are subject to the risks of the Japanese economy and currency exchange rates.

Eurobonds: These bonds are issued by entities outside of the country in which they are denominated, typically in the Eurodollar market. They are subject to the risks of currency exchange rates.

Catastrophe bonds: These bonds are designed to provide insurance coverage for natural disasters or other catastrophic events. They offer the potential for higher returns but also come with the risk of the event not occurring or not being severe enough to trigger a payout.

Hybrid bonds: These bonds have characteristics of both debt and equity, such as convertible bonds or bonds with profit-sharing provisions. They offer the potential for higher returns but also come with the risk of the equity component not performing as expected.

Green bonds: These bonds are issued by entities to finance environmentally friendly projects, such as renewable energy or energy efficiency improvements. They are generally considered to be less risky than other types of bonds because they are backed by projects with a positive social impact.

In conclusion, there are many different types of bonds available to investors, each with their own unique risks and potential rewards. It is important for investors to carefully consider their investment goals and risk tolerance before choosing which type of bond to invest in. By understanding the different types of bonds and their risks, investors can make informed decisions to help them achieve their financial goals.

How to Buy and Sell Bonds

Understand the bond market: Before buying or selling bonds, it's essential to understand the bond market. The bond market is a market where investors buy and sell bonds, which are essentially loans made to companies or governments.

⬚ Determine your investment goals: You need to determine your investment goals before buying or selling bonds. Are you looking for income or capital appreciation? This will help you decide which bonds to buy or sell.

⬚ Research bonds: Researching bonds is essential before buying or selling. Look for bonds that fit your investment goals and have a good credit rating.

⬚ Decide on the type of bonds: There are many types of bonds, including government bonds, corporate bonds, municipal bonds, and high-yield bonds. Each type has different risks and rewards.

⬚ Decide on the maturity of the bond: Bonds have different maturities, ranging from short-term (less than one year) to long-term (30 years or more). Longer-term bonds usually offer higher interest rates but carry more risk.

⬚ Choose a broker: You need a broker to buy or sell bonds. Look for a broker with a good reputation and reasonable fees.

⬚ Open an account: Once you've chosen a broker, you need to open an account. The broker will require personal and financial information, and you'll need to fund the account.

⬚ Place an order: To buy or sell bonds, you need to place an order with your broker. The order will include the type of bond, the quantity, and the price.

⬚ Monitor the market: The bond market can be volatile, so it's essential to monitor the market regularly.

⬚ Use limit orders: When placing an order, use limit orders to ensure you get the price you want. A limit order specifies the maximum price you're willing to pay to buy or the minimum price you're willing to accept to sell.

⬚ Understand yield: Yield is the return on investment for a bond. It's essential to understand yield before buying or selling bonds.

⬚ Consider the coupon rate: The coupon rate is the interest rate paid on a bond. It's essential to consider the coupon rate before buying or selling bonds.

⬚ Look for discounts and premiums: Bonds can be sold at a discount or a premium. Look for bonds selling at a discount to get a better yield.

⬚ Consider tax implications: Bonds have tax implications. Municipal bonds are usually tax-free, while others may be subject to federal and state taxes.

⬚ Consider inflation: Inflation can affect the value of bonds. Look for bonds with inflation protection to ensure your investment maintains its value.

⬚ Understand credit ratings: Credit ratings indicate the creditworthiness of a bond issuer.

It's essential to consider credit ratings before buying or selling bonds.

☐ Consider diversification: Diversification is essential when buying or selling bonds. Look for bonds with different maturities, yields, and credit ratings to minimize risk.

☐ Understand callable bonds: Callable bonds can be redeemed early by the issuer. It's essential to consider callable bonds before buying or selling.

☐ Consider bond funds: Bond funds can provide diversification and professional management. Look for bond funds with low fees and a good track record.

☐ Understand bid-ask spread: The bid-ask spread is the difference between the buying and selling price of a bond. It's essential to consider the bid-ask spread before buying or selling bonds.

☐ Monitor your bonds: Once you've bought bonds, it's essential to monitor them regularly. Look for changes in credit ratings, interest rates, and market conditions.

☐ Sell bonds at maturity: When a bond reaches maturity, it's redeemed for its face value. It's usually best to sell bonds at maturity, as this ensures you get the full value of the bond.

☐ Sell bonds before maturity: You may want to sell bonds before maturity if interest rates rise, as this can reduce the value of your bonds. However, this can also result in a loss if you sell below the face value.

☐ Consider market conditions: Market conditions can affect the value of bonds. Look for opportunities to buy or sell when market conditions are favorable.

☐ Seek professional advice: Buying and selling bonds can be complex. If you're unsure about buying or selling bonds, seek professional advice from a financial advisor. A financial advisor can help you understand the risks and rewards of investing in bonds and develop a bond investment strategy that aligns with your investment goals.

CHAPTER 4: THE IMPORTANCE OF ASSET ALLOCATION

What Is Asset Allocation?

Asset allocation is the process of dividing your investment portfolio among different types of assets such as stocks, bonds, cash, and real estate.

The purpose of asset allocation is to create a balanced and diversified investment portfolio that can help you achieve your financial goals while minimizing risk.

Asset allocation takes into account your investment objectives, risk tolerance, and time horizon.

The right asset allocation strategy will depend on your unique financial situation, and may require adjustments over time.

Asset allocation is not a one-time decision, but rather an ongoing process that requires monitoring and occasional rebalancing.

The key to successful asset allocation is to maintain a well-diversified portfolio that can weather market volatility and provide long-term growth.

Asset allocation can help you reduce the impact of market downturns on your investment portfolio by spreading your risk across multiple asset classes.

It can also help you take advantage of potential growth opportunities in different areas of the market.

Asset allocation is an important tool for managing risk and maximizing returns over the long term.

By diversifying your portfolio across different asset classes, you can potentially achieve a better risk-adjusted return than if you invested solely in one asset class.

How to Determine Your Asset Allocation Strategy

The first step in determining your asset allocation strategy is to identify your investment goals and objectives.

Your investment goals will help guide your asset allocation decisions, such as how much risk you're willing to take on and how long you have to invest.

Next, you'll need to assess your risk tolerance, or your willingness to accept market volatility and potential losses in exchange for potential gains.

Your risk tolerance will help you determine the appropriate mix of assets in your portfolio.

Younger investors with a longer time horizon may be more willing to take on riskier investments, such as stocks, in order to achieve higher long-term returns.

Older investors nearing retirement may prefer a more conservative investment strategy, with a higher allocation to fixed-income investments.

Once you've determined your investment goals and risk tolerance, you can start building your investment portfolio.

A well-diversified portfolio should include a mix of assets such as stocks, bonds, cash, and real estate.

The specific asset allocation that's right for you will depend on a variety of factors, including your age, income, and overall financial situation.

You may want to consider working with a financial advisor to help you determine the right asset allocation strategy for your needs.

It's important to periodically review and rebalance your portfolio to ensure it remains aligned with your investment goals and objectives.

Rebalancing involves adjusting your portfolio back to its original asset allocation mix, which can help you maintain your desired risk level and potential returns.

Asset allocation can help you achieve your financial goals while minimizing risk, but it's important to remember that no investment strategy is foolproof.

It's important to understand the risks associated with each asset class and to invest with a long-term perspective.

A well-designed asset allocation strategy can help you achieve financial stability and growth over the long term.

By diversifying your investments and maintaining a disciplined approach to investing, you can potentially achieve your financial goals while minimizing risk.

Asset allocation can help you take advantage of potential growth opportunities in different areas of the market while reducing the impact of market downturns on your portfolio.

A disciplined and well-diversified approach to asset allocation can help you achieve financial security and peace of mind.

It's important to periodically review and adjust your asset allocation strategy as your financial situation and investment goals change over time.

An important factor to consider when determining your asset allocation strategy is your investment time horizon, or the length of time you have to invest.

Investors with a longer time horizon may be more willing to take on riskier investments, such as stocks, because they have more time to recover from market downturns.

Investors with a shorter time horizon may prefer a more conservative investment strategy, with a higher allocation to fixed-income investments, to help preserve their capital.

It's important to balance your desire for potential returns with your need to protect your capital, based on your individual investment goals and time horizon.

Asset allocation should also take into account your current financial situation, including your income, expenses, and debt.

Your asset allocation strategy may need to be adjusted if your financial situation changes, such as a loss of income or unexpected expenses.

In addition to diversifying your portfolio among different asset classes, you may also want to consider diversifying within each asset class.

For example, within the stock portion of your portfolio, you may want to consider investing in a mix of large-cap, mid-cap, and small-cap stocks to achieve a well-diversified portfolio.

Similarly, within the bond portion of your portfolio, you may want to consider investing in a mix of short-term, intermediate-term, and long-term bonds to achieve a well-diversified portfolio.

A well-diversified portfolio can help you reduce the impact of individual stock or bond performance on your overall portfolio returns.

Another important factor to consider when determining your asset allocation strategy is the correlation between different asset classes.

Correlation refers to the degree to which different asset classes move in the same direction at the same time.

By investing in asset classes with low correlation, you can potentially reduce your overall portfolio risk and volatility.

For example, stocks and bonds tend to have low correlation, meaning that when one asset class is performing poorly, the other may be performing well.

Real estate and commodities are also asset classes that may have low correlation with stocks and bonds, and may be worth considering as part of a diversified portfolio.

It's important to remember that no asset allocation strategy is foolproof, and all investments carry some degree of risk.

The key to successful investing is to maintain a well-diversified portfolio and to invest with a long-term perspective.

Regularly reviewing and adjusting your asset allocation strategy can help ensure that your portfolio remains aligned with your investment goals and risk tolerance.

In addition to diversifying your portfolio, you may also want to consider investing in low-cost index funds or exchange-traded funds (ETFs) to help keep your investment costs low.

By following a disciplined approach to asset allocation and investing, you can potentially achieve your financial goals and build a secure financial future.

CHAPTER 5: HOW TO BUILD A DIVERSIFIED PORTFOLIO

Why Diversification Is Important:

Diversification is crucial to any investment strategy because it helps to minimize risk. By spreading your money across a range of different asset classes and investment types, you can reduce the impact of any one investment's poor performance on your overall portfolio.

Diversification also allows you to capture the potential upside of different types of investments. While some investments may be performing poorly, others may be doing well, balancing out your returns and potentially earning you more in the long run.

Another benefit of diversification is that it can help you avoid making emotional investment decisions. When you have all your money in one investment or asset class, it can be tempting to panic when that investment starts to lose value. Diversification helps you stay level-headed and focused on your long-term investment goals.

In addition to minimizing risk, diversification can also help you achieve your financial goals more quickly. By investing in a variety of asset classes with different risk levels and potential returns, you can potentially earn higher returns over time without taking on excessive risk.

Diversification can also help you align your investments with your values. For example, if you're passionate about supporting sustainable businesses, you might choose to invest in companies that prioritize environmental and social responsibility.

How to Choose the Right Investments for Your Portfolio:

- Start by assessing your risk tolerance. Before you invest any money, it's important to understand how much risk you're comfortable taking on. This will help you determine the types of investments that are right for you.
- Consider your investment goals. Are you saving for a short-term or long-term goal? Do you need to generate income from your investments, or are you looking for growth potential? Your investment goals should guide your investment decisions.
- Research different types of investments. There are many different types of investments, including stocks, bonds, mutual funds, exchange-traded funds (ETFs), real estate, and more. Each type of investment has its own unique risk and return profile, so it's important to understand the pros and cons of each.
- Determine the appropriate asset allocation for your portfolio. Once you've assessed your risk tolerance and investment goals, you can determine the right mix of asset classes for your portfolio. This will help you achieve a balance between risk and return that aligns with your goals and risk tolerance.
- Consider using index funds or ETFs. These types of investments can provide broad exposure to a range of asset classes, making it easy to achieve diversification within your portfolio.
- Evaluate the fees and expenses associated with each investment. Fees can eat into your investment returns, so it's important to choose investments with reasonable fees and expenses.
- Stay diversified over time. Your asset allocation may shift over time as some investments perform better than others. It's important to periodically evaluate your portfolio and rebalance as needed to maintain a well-diversified portfolio.
- Consider consulting with a financial advisor. If you're unsure about how to choose the right investments for your portfolio or how to diversify effectively, consider seeking the advice of a financial professional who can help guide you through the process.
- Be aware of your tax situation. Taxes can impact your investment returns, so it's important to consider the tax implications of your investment decisions.
- Remember that diversification doesn't guarantee a profit or protect against losses. While diversification is an important part of any investment strategy, it's important to remember that it doesn't guarantee a profit or protect against losses. The key is to maintain a well-diversified portfolio that aligns with your risk tolerance and investment goals

CHAPTER 6: INVESTING FOR RETIREMENT

Understanding Retirement Accounts:

Retirement accounts are a type of investment account that is designed to help individuals save for their retirement. These accounts offer tax benefits that can help individuals save money on their taxes and maximize their retirement savings. There are several types of retirement accounts, including 401(k) plans, Individual Retirement Accounts (IRAs), and Roth IRAs.

How 401(k) Plans Work:

A 401(k) plan is a type of retirement savings plan that is sponsored by employers. It allows employees to contribute a portion of their salary on a pre-tax basis, which can help reduce their taxable income.

The money that employees contribute to their 401(k) plan is invested in a variety of financial products, such as mutual funds, stocks, and bonds. This means that the value of their account can go up or down depending on the performance of these investments.

Employers may also offer a matching contribution to their employees' 401(k) plans. This means that they will match a certain percentage of the employee's contribution, up to a certain limit. This can be a significant benefit, as it can help increase the employee's retirement savings.

In general, employees are eligible to participate in their employer's 401(k) plan if they are at least 21 years old and have worked for the company for a certain amount of time. However, some employers may have additional eligibility requirements.

Employees can typically contribute up to a certain percentage of their salary to their 401(k) plan each year, with a maximum limit set by the IRS. In 2023, the maximum contribution limit is $20,500, but it may be adjusted in future years.

One advantage of a 401(k) plan is that contributions are made on a pre-tax basis, which means that the employee's taxable income is reduced. This can result in a lower tax bill each year.

However, when employees withdraw money from their 401(k) plan in retirement, they will have to pay taxes on the withdrawals. This means that they may not save as much in taxes as they initially thought.

Employees can typically choose from a variety of investment options when contributing to their 401(k) plan. This can include mutual funds, target-date funds, and individual stocks and bonds. The investment options available may vary depending on the employer.

One important thing to keep in mind is that investments in a 401(k) plan are not guaranteed. The value of the account can go up or down depending on the performance of the investments.

Another important consideration is fees. 401(k) plans typically have fees associated with them, which can vary depending on the plan. It's important to understand these fees and how they may impact the overall performance of the account.

Employees can typically make changes to their 401(k) contributions and investments at any time. This can include increasing or decreasing their contributions, as well as changing the investments they are invested in.

It's important to remember that contributions to a 401(k) plan are subject to certain annual limits. If an employee reaches the annual limit before the end of the year, they will not be able to contribute any more money until the next year.

Some employers may offer a Roth 401(k) option, which allows employees to contribute after-tax dollars to their retirement account. This means that withdrawals in retirement will be tax-free.

Another important feature of 401(k) plans is vesting. Vesting refers to the employee's ownership of the employer's contributions to the plan. In some cases, employees may not be fully vested in the employer's contributions until they have worked for the company for a certain amount of time.

In general, employees can begin withdrawing money from their 401(k) plan without penalty once they reach age 59 1/2. However, withdrawals made before this age may be subject to a 10% early withdrawal penalty, in addition to taxes.

Some employers may offer a loan option for their 401(k) plan. This allows employees to borrow money from their retirement account, with interest. However, taking a loan from a 401(k) plan can have significant drawbacks. For one, the money that is borrowed is no longer invested in the account, which can impact the employee's retirement savings. Additionally, if the employee is unable to pay back the loan, it may be treated as an early withdrawal and subject to taxes and penalties.

When an employee leaves their job, they may have the option to roll over their 401(k) account to a new employer's plan or an individual retirement account (IRA). Rolling over the account can help avoid taxes and penalties associated with early withdrawals.

If an employee does not roll over their 401(k) account and instead withdraws the money, they may be subject to taxes and penalties. Additionally, they may miss out on the potential for continued investment growth in the account.

It's important to review the investment options available in a 401(k) plan and make informed decisions about how to allocate contributions. This may include diversifying investments across a variety of asset classes and considering the employee's risk tolerance and investment goals.

Another important factor to consider is the employee's overall financial situation. While saving for retirement is important, it may be necessary to prioritize other financial goals, such as paying off debt or building an emergency fund.

Employers may also offer a Roth 401(k) option, which allows employees to contribute after-tax dollars to their retirement account. This means that withdrawals in retirement will be tax-free.

One key advantage of a Roth 401(k) is that it can provide tax diversification in retirement. This means that the employee will have both tax-free and taxable sources of income, which can help reduce the overall tax burden.

However, contributing to a Roth 401(k) may not be the best option for everyone. It's important to consider factors such as the employee's current tax rate and expected tax rate in retirement.

In some cases, employers may also offer a profit-sharing contribution to their employees' 401(k) plan. This means that the employer will contribute a certain percentage of profits to the plan, which can be a significant benefit to employees.

Employees may also be able to make catch-up contributions to their 401(k) plan once they reach age 50. This can help increase their retirement savings as they approach retirement age.

It's important to review the performance of a 401(k) plan on a regular basis and make any necessary adjustments to contributions and investments. This can help ensure that the employee is on track to meet their retirement goals.

Some employers may also offer financial education and planning resources to their employees. This can be a valuable resource for those who may be unfamiliar with the ins and outs of 401(k) plans and retirement savings.

In summary, 401(k) plans are a popular retirement savings option that offer a number of advantages, including tax benefits, employer matching contributions, and a variety of investment options. However, it's important to carefully consider factors such as fees, investment options, and overall financial goals when contributing to a 401(k) plan.

With careful planning and attention to detail, employees can use a 401(k) plan to build a solid foundation for their retirement savings and achieve their financial goals.

Devon R. Blackwell

How to Maximize Your 401(k) Savings:

Start by enrolling in your company's 401(k) plan as soon as you're eligible. This will help ensure that you can take advantage of the plan's benefits right away and start saving for your future retirement.

Contribute as much as you can to your 401(k) plan. While the maximum contribution limits change every year, it's generally a good idea to contribute as much as possible to get the most out of your retirement savings.

Consider contributing enough to your 401(k) to take advantage of your employer's matching program. Many employers offer matching contributions to encourage their employees to save for retirement, so it's important to take advantage of this benefit.

Review your 401(k) plan's investment options carefully. Look for funds with low fees and a solid track record of performance over time. Diversify your investments by choosing a mix of stocks, bonds, and other assets that align with your retirement goals.

Don't forget about the power of compound interest. Even small contributions can add up over time, so start saving early and make regular contributions to your 401(k) plan.

Avoid taking early withdrawals from your 401(k) plan, as these can result in penalties and taxes that can eat into your retirement savings. Instead, focus on contributing consistently and sticking to your long-term retirement goals.

Consider increasing your contributions over time. As your income grows, you may be able to afford to contribute more to your 401(k) plan, which can help maximize your retirement savings over time.

Be aware of the contribution limits for your 401(k) plan. If you hit the limit, you may want to consider other retirement savings options, such as a traditional or Roth IRA.

Stay up to date on changes to your 401(k) plan, including changes to contribution limits, investment options, and other plan features that can impact your retirement savings.

Take advantage of automatic contributions if your 401(k) plan offers them. This can help you save consistently and avoid the temptation to spend money on other things.

Consider consulting with a financial advisor to help you make informed decisions about your 401(k) plan and other retirement savings options.

Look for ways to reduce your expenses so that you can contribute more to your 401(k) plan. This might include cutting back on unnecessary expenses, such as eating out or buying expensive clothes.

Avoid making emotional decisions about your 401(k) plan, such as selling all of your investments during a market downturn. Instead, stay the course and stick to your long-term retirement goals.

Be aware of any fees associated with your 401(k) plan, including administrative fees and investment fees. These fees can eat into your retirement savings over time, so it's important to understand them and look for ways to minimize them.

Consider taking advantage of catch-up contributions if you're over 50. This can help you boost your retirement savings in the years leading up to your retirement.

Be aware of the tax implications of your 401(k) plan. Contributions to a traditional 401(k) plan are tax-deferred, which means you'll pay taxes on the money when you withdraw it in retirement. Contributions to a Roth 401(k) plan, on the other hand, are made with after-tax dollars, which means you won't pay taxes on the money when you withdraw it in retirement.

Consider rebalancing your portfolio periodically to ensure that your investments are aligned with your retirement goals. This might involve selling some investments and buying others to maintain the right mix of assets in your portfolio.

Don't forget about the importance of emergency savings. While it's important to save for retirement, it's also important to have some money set aside for unexpected expenses, such as car repairs or medical bills. Having an emergency fund can help prevent you from having to dip into your retirement savings in a pinch.

Make sure to review your 401(k) plan regularly to ensure that it's still meeting your needs and goals. If your retirement goals or financial situation changes, you may need to adjust your contributions or investment strategy accordingly.

Finally, don't be afraid to seek out resources and support to help you maximize your 401(k) savings. This might include attending financial planning seminars, talking to a financial advisor, or connecting with other individuals who are also working to build their retirement savings. By staying informed and connected, you can maximize your 401(k) savings and achieve your long-term retirement goals.

Understanding Traditional IRAs:

An Individual Retirement Account (IRA) is a type of savings account that allows individuals to save money for their retirement. Traditional IRAs are one of the most popular types of IRAs.

Traditional IRAs are tax-deferred retirement accounts, which means that you don't pay taxes on the money you contribute to the account until you withdraw it during retirement.

Anyone who earns income can contribute to a traditional IRA, regardless of age, as long as they don't exceed the annual contribution limit set by the IRS.

Traditional IRAs have contribution limits that are adjusted each year for inflation. As of 2021, the contribution limit is $6,000 per year for individuals under age 50 and $7,000 per year for individuals age 50 and older.

The money you contribute to a traditional IRA is tax-deductible, which means that you can deduct the amount of your contributions from your taxable income.

Traditional IRAs offer a range of investment options, including stocks, bonds, mutual funds, and other types of investments.

One advantage of traditional IRAs is that they offer tax-deferred growth. This means that your money can grow tax-free until you withdraw it during retirement.

Withdrawals from traditional IRAs are taxed as ordinary income, which means that you'll pay income taxes on the money you withdraw.

Traditional IRAs have required minimum distributions (RMDs), which means that you're required to take a certain amount of money out of your account each year starting at age 72.

Traditional IRAs can be opened at banks, credit unions, brokerage firms, and other financial institutions.

If you withdraw money from your traditional IRA before age 59 ½, you'll typically have to pay a 10% early withdrawal penalty in addition to income taxes.

Traditional IRAs can be converted to Roth IRAs, which are a type of retirement account that offers tax-free growth and tax-free withdrawals during retirement.

Traditional IRAs are often used by individuals who expect to be in a lower tax bracket during retirement than they are currently.

You can make contributions to a traditional IRA for the previous tax year up until the tax-filing deadline, which is typically April 15th.

Traditional IRAs can be inherited by your beneficiaries, but the rules for inherited IRAs can be complicated.

If you're married and don't have earned income, you can still contribute to a traditional IRA as long as your spouse has earned income and you file taxes jointly.

Traditional IRAs can be used to fund a variety of retirement expenses, including healthcare costs, travel, and hobbies.

Traditional IRAs can be rolled over into other retirement accounts, such as 401(k)s or other types of

IRAs.

Traditional IRAs are subject to certain contribution limits and income limits. If you exceed these limits, you may be subject to penalties.

Traditional IRAs offer a number of tax benefits and investment options, but it's important to consult with a financial advisor to determine if a traditional IRA is the right retirement savings account for you.

Understanding Roth IRAs:

A Roth IRA is a retirement savings account that allows individuals to contribute post-tax income and withdraw funds tax-free after age 59 and a half.

Roth IRAs were created in 1997 by the Taxpayer Relief Act and are named after their chief legislative sponsor, Senator William Roth of Delaware.

Unlike traditional IRAs, Roth IRAs do not offer a tax deduction for contributions, but they provide a tax-free source of income during retirement.

Contributions to a Roth IRA are limited to $6,000 per year for individuals under 50, and $7,000 for those over 50. This limit is subject to change depending on inflation rates.

There are income limits for contributing to a Roth IRA. For individuals, the limit for 2021 is $140,000 for single filers and $208,000 for married couples filing jointly. Above these thresholds, contribution limits are phased out.

Roth IRAs offer several advantages, such as tax-free growth, no required minimum distributions, and the ability to withdraw contributions penalty-free at any time.

Contributions to a Roth IRA are made with after-tax dollars, so there is no immediate tax benefit. However, when you withdraw money from your account, it is tax-free.

Unlike traditional IRAs, Roth IRAs do not require you to take required minimum distributions (RMDs) at age 72, so your money can continue to grow tax-free for as long as you want.

If you need to withdraw funds from your Roth IRA before age 59 and a half, you may be subject to taxes and penalties on the earnings portion of the withdrawal. However, you can withdraw your contributions at any time without penalty.

You can open a Roth IRA with a brokerage firm, bank, or other financial institution. It is important to shop around for the best rates and fees.

You can invest your Roth IRA in a variety of assets, including stocks, bonds, mutual funds, and exchange-traded funds (ETFs).

It is important to choose your investments carefully, as the performance of your portfolio will determine the growth of your retirement savings.

You can also convert a traditional IRA to a Roth IRA, but you will have to pay taxes on the converted amount.

Roth IRAs are a good option for those who expect to be in a higher tax bracket during retirement than they are now.

Roth IRAs can also be used to leave a tax-free inheritance to your heirs.

If you have both a traditional and a Roth IRA, you can withdraw from either or both accounts to meet your retirement income needs.

Roth IRAs are not subject to required minimum distributions during your lifetime, but they are subject to RMDs after your death, unless you leave them to a qualified charity.

Roth IRAs can be a valuable tool for retirement planning, but they are not suitable for everyone. It is important to consult with a financial advisor to determine if a Roth IRA is the right choice for you.

Roth IRAs offer a tax-free source of income during retirement, which can help you maintain your standard of living without having to worry about taxes eating away at your savings.

By understanding Roth IRAs, you can make informed decisions about your retirement savings and ensure that you have a secure financial future.

Devon R. Blackwell

How to Choose Between a Traditional and Roth IRA:

Choosing between a Traditional IRA and a Roth IRA is an important decision when it comes to planning for your retirement. Here are some factors to consider to help you make the best choice for your specific situation:

Consider your current tax bracket: If you are in a higher tax bracket now than you expect to be in retirement, it may make sense to contribute to a Traditional IRA and take advantage of the tax deduction now.

Think about your future tax bracket: If you expect to be in a higher tax bracket in retirement than you are now, a Roth IRA may be a better choice since you pay taxes on the contributions now, and withdrawals in retirement are tax-free.

Look at your income limits: Keep in mind that there are income limits for contributing to a Roth IRA, so if your income is above the limit, a Traditional IRA may be your only option.

Consider your time horizon: If you have a long time horizon before retirement, a Roth IRA may be a better choice since your contributions have more time to grow tax-free.

Think about your future income needs: If you anticipate needing to withdraw money from your IRA in retirement to cover your living expenses, a Traditional IRA may be a better choice since you may be in a lower tax bracket in retirement.

Consider your current and future investment income: If you have a lot of other investment income now or expect to have significant investment income in retirement, a Traditional IRA may be better since it reduces your current taxable income.

Think about your estate planning needs: If you plan to leave your IRA to your heirs, a Roth IRA may be a better choice since withdrawals by your heirs are tax-free.

Look at the fees and expenses associated with each type of IRA: Make sure to compare the fees and expenses associated with each type of IRA to determine which is the most cost-effective option for you.

Consider the impact of required minimum distributions: If you are age 72 or older, you are required to take minimum distributions from your Traditional IRA each year, which may impact your tax situation. A Roth IRA does not have required minimum distributions.

Think about your risk tolerance: If you are risk-averse, a Traditional IRA may be a better choice since you can deduct contributions now and reduce your taxable income.

Consider your future financial goals: If you anticipate having significant financial needs in retirement, a Roth IRA may be a better choice since you can withdraw contributions tax-free.

Look at your other retirement accounts: If you already have a 401(k) or other retirement accounts, it may make sense to diversify your retirement savings by choosing a Roth IRA.

Think about your employer's retirement plan: If your employer offers a retirement plan, such as a 401(k), make sure to consider how that plan fits into your overall retirement strategy.

Look at your contribution limits: Keep in mind that the contribution limits for each type of IRA may impact your decision. For 2023, the contribution limit for both Traditional and Roth IRAs is $6,000, or

$7,000 if you are age 50 or older.

Consider your overall tax situation: Think about how contributing to either a Traditional or Roth IRA may impact your overall tax situation, including your taxable income and deductions.

Think about your investment strategy: Consider your investment strategy and how it fits with the tax benefits of each type of IRA. For example, if you plan to invest in high-growth stocks, a Roth IRA may be a better choice.

Look at the potential for future tax law changes: Keep in mind that tax laws can change, so make sure to consider the potential impact of any future changes on your IRA choice.

Think about your retirement timeline: If you plan to retire early, a Roth IRA may be a better choice since you can withdraw contributions tax-free at any time without penalty.

Consider your future health care costs: If you anticipate significant health care costs in retirement, a Traditional IRA may be a better choice since withdrawals for medical expenses are penalty-free.

Think about your expected Social Security benefits: If you expect to receive significant Social Security benefits in retirement, a Traditional IRA may be a better choice since withdrawals can be coordinated with your Social Security benefits to minimize your tax liability.

Look at the flexibility of each type of IRA: Consider the flexibility of each type of IRA, including the ability to withdraw contributions penalty-free from a Roth IRA and the ability to convert a Traditional IRA to a Roth IRA.

Think about the impact of inflation: Keep in mind the impact of inflation on your retirement savings and consider which type of IRA may better protect your savings from inflation.

Consider your current and future debt: If you have significant debt now or expect to have significant debt in retirement, a Traditional IRA may be a better choice since you can deduct contributions now and reduce your taxable income.

Look at your overall financial situation: Consider your overall financial situation, including your income, expenses, and debt, to determine which type of IRA may be the most beneficial for you.

Think about your risk capacity: Consider your risk capacity, or your ability to withstand market volatility and risk, when choosing between a Traditional and Roth IRA.

Consult with a financial advisor: It is always a good idea to consult with a financial advisor who can help you evaluate your specific situation and make the best choice for your retirement savings.

Understanding SEP IRAs:

A Simplified Employee Pension Individual Retirement Account (SEP IRA) is a type of retirement account that is available to self-employed individuals and small business owners. Here are some key points to help you better understand SEP IRAs:

A SEP IRA is a tax-deferred retirement account that allows self-employed individuals and small business owners to contribute money towards their retirement.

Contributions to a SEP IRA are tax-deductible, which means that they can reduce your taxable income and lower your tax bill.

SEP IRAs are only available to employers with fewer than 25 employees, although the employer does not have to contribute to each employee's account.

Employees are not allowed to make contributions to a SEP IRA, only the employer can make contributions on behalf of the employee.

The employer is not required to make contributions every year and can adjust the amount of contributions from year to year.

The maximum contribution limit for a SEP IRA is the lesser of 25% of compensation or $61,000 for 2022.

Contributions to a SEP IRA must be made by the employer's tax-filing deadline, including extensions.

SEP IRAs have no age limit for contributions, so employers can continue to contribute to an employee's account even after they reach age 70 ½.

Withdrawals from a SEP IRA are taxed as regular income, and a 10% penalty may apply if you withdraw funds before age 59 ½.

The required minimum distribution (RMD) rules apply to SEP IRAs, which means that you must begin taking distributions from your account by age 72.

SEP IRAs can be opened and managed by most financial institutions, including banks, brokerage firms, and mutual fund companies.

SEP IRAs can be invested in a variety of assets, including stocks, bonds, mutual funds, and exchange-traded funds (ETFs).

SEP IRAs can be used in combination with other types of retirement accounts, such as a 401(k) or a Traditional IRA.

SEP IRAs are often used by self-employed individuals and small business owners because they are relatively easy to set up and have low administrative costs.

SEP IRAs are not subject to the same contribution limits as Traditional and Roth IRAs, which makes them a good option for those who want to save more for retirement.

SEP IRAs are not subject to the same contribution limits as 401(k)s, which can make them a good option for small business owners who want to save more for retirement than they can with a 401(k).

SEP IRAs are not subject to the same testing requirements as 401(k)s, which makes them a simpler and less expensive option for small business owners.

SEP IRAs do not require the same level of ongoing administrative work as a 401(k) plan, which can save time and money for small business owners.

SEP IRAs can be a good option for businesses with fluctuating income because contributions can be adjusted from year to year.

SEP IRAs can be a good option for businesses with high-profit margins because the employer can contribute up to 25% of compensation.

SEP IRAs can be a good option for businesses that want to incentivize employee retention because the employer can contribute to an employee's account even if they are no longer with the company.

SEP IRAs can be a good option for businesses that want to avoid the costs and complexity of a 401(k) plan but still want to offer a retirement savings option to their employees.

SEP IRAs can be a good option for self-employed individuals who want to save more for retirement than they can with a Traditional or Roth IRA.

SEP IRAs with any retirement account, it's important to understand the fees associated with a SEP IRA, including account maintenance fees, transaction fees, and investment fees.

It's important to work with a financial advisor who can help you determine if a SEP IRA is the best retirement savings option for you and your business, as well as help you navigate the rules and regulations associated with this type of account.

In conclusion, a SEP IRA can be a valuable retirement savings option for self-employed individuals and small business owners who want to save more for retirement and take advantage of tax-deductible contributions. However, it's important to carefully consider your options and work with a financial advisor to determine if a SEP IRA is the best choice for your business and your retirement goals. With careful planning and management, a SEP IRA can help you build a secure retirement future.

How to Maximize Your SEP IRA Savings:

A Simplified Employee Pension (SEP) IRA is a retirement savings plan that is specifically designed for small business owners and self-employed individuals. If you have a SEP IRA, here are some tips to help you maximize your savings:

Make the maximum contribution: For 2023, you can contribute up to 25% of your compensation or $61,000, whichever is less, to your SEP IRA. Make sure to contribute the maximum amount if you are able to do so.

Establish the plan as early as possible: The earlier you establish your SEP IRA plan, the more time your contributions have to grow and accumulate tax-free.

Consider contributing more than the minimum required amount: Although you are only required to contribute a minimum of 2% of your employee's compensation to a SEP IRA, you may want to consider contributing more to attract and retain top talent.

Choose the right investment strategy: Choose an investment strategy that aligns with your risk tolerance and long-term retirement goals.

Consider consolidating your retirement accounts: Consolidating your retirement accounts can help you save on fees and simplify your retirement planning.

Review your plan annually: Review your SEP IRA plan annually to make sure it is still meeting your needs and goals.

Use catch-up contributions: If you are 50 or older, you can make catch-up contributions of up to $6,500 in addition to the maximum contribution limit.

Contribute early in the year: Contribute to your SEP IRA as early in the year as possible to give your contributions more time to grow.

Consider the impact of taxes: Keep in mind the impact of taxes on your contributions and plan accordingly to minimize your tax liability.

Automate your contributions: Automating your SEP IRA contributions can help ensure that you are consistently saving for retirement.

Consider the impact of inflation: Keep in mind the impact of inflation on your retirement savings and adjust your contributions accordingly.

Educate yourself about your SEP IRA plan: Learn as much as you can about your SEP IRA plan to make sure you are making the most of your savings opportunities.

Coordinate your SEP IRA with your Social Security benefits: Coordinate your SEP IRA contributions with your Social Security benefits to help minimize your tax liability in retirement.

Choose the right plan administrator: Choose a plan administrator that has the expertise and experience to help you maximize your SEP IRA savings.

Keep track of your contributions: Keep detailed records of your SEP IRA contributions and ensure that you are in compliance with all applicable regulations.

Consider the impact of required minimum distributions: Keep in mind that you are required to take required minimum distributions (RMDs) from your SEP IRA starting at age 72. Plan accordingly to ensure that you are able to meet your RMD obligations.

Consider the impact of penalties: Keep in mind that early withdrawals from your SEP IRA are subject to penalties, so plan accordingly to avoid unnecessary penalties.

Diversify your investments: Diversifying your investments can help reduce your overall risk and improve your chances of achieving your retirement goals.

Consider the impact of fees: Keep in mind the impact of fees on your SEP IRA savings and choose investments and plan administrators that offer low fees.

Review your plan with your financial advisor: Review your SEP IRA plan with your financial advisor regularly to ensure that you are on track to meet your retirement goals.

Coordinate your SEP IRA with other retirement accounts: Coordinate your SEP IRA contributions with contributions to other retirement accounts, such as a 401(k), to maximize your overall retirement savings.

Use employer matching contributions: If you offer employer matching contributions to your employees, make sure to take advantage of these contributions yourself.

Plan for unexpected expenses: Plan for unexpected expenses and emergencies by setting aside additional savings in a separate emergency fund.

Consider the impact of market volatility: Keep in mind the impact of market volatility on your SEP IRA savings and adjust your investment strategy accordingly.

Educate your employees about the SEP IRA plan: Educate your employees about the benefits of the SEP IRA plan and encourage them to contribute to maximize their retirement savings.

Review your plan periodically: Review your SEP IRA plan periodically to ensure that it is still the best retirement savings option for you and your employees. Consider other retirement savings plans if your needs change or if a different plan better meets your needs.

By following these tips, you can maximize your SEP IRA savings and ensure that you are on track to achieve your retirement goals. Remember to consult with your financial advisor to ensure that your SEP IRA plan is in line with your overall retirement savings strategy. With careful planning and consistent contributions, you can build a robust retirement savings nest egg and enjoy a secure retirement.

Devon R. Blackwell

Understanding Simple IRAs:

A Simple IRA, or Savings Incentive Match Plan for Employees, is a retirement plan that can be set up by small businesses with up to 100 employees. Here are some things to understand about Simple IRAs:

Eligibility: To be eligible for a Simple IRA, you must have earned income and work for a business that has set up the plan.

Contributions: Both the employer and the employee can make contributions to a Simple IRA. The employer must either match employee contributions up to a certain percentage of their salary or contribute a flat 2% of all eligible employees' salaries, even if the employee does not contribute.

Contribution Limits: In 2023, the contribution limit for a Simple IRA is $13,500 for employees under age 50 and $16,500 for those 50 and older. Employer contributions do not count towards these limits.

Tax Benefits: Contributions to a Simple IRA are tax-deductible for both the employer and the employee. Earnings on contributions grow tax-deferred until withdrawals are made in retirement.

Vesting: Employee contributions are always 100% vested, but employer contributions may be subject to a vesting schedule that requires the employee to work for a certain period of time before the contributions are fully vested.

Withdrawals: Withdrawals from a Simple IRA are subject to income tax and may be subject to a 10% early withdrawal penalty if taken before age 59 1/2, unless an exception applies.

Rollovers: A Simple IRA can be rolled over into another Simple IRA or a Traditional IRA, but not a Roth IRA.

Investment Options: Simple IRAs may offer a range of investment options, such as mutual funds or exchange-traded funds, depending on the plan's sponsor.

Employee Participation: Employee participation in a Simple IRA is voluntary, but the employer must offer the plan to all eligible employees.

Plan Administration: The employer is responsible for administering the plan, including setting up the plan, making contributions, and ensuring compliance with IRS rules and regulations.

Employer Requirements: Employers must provide employees with a Summary Plan Description (SPD) that outlines the plan's features, eligibility requirements, contribution limits, and withdrawal rules.

Deadlines: Employers must establish the plan by October 1 of the calendar year in which the plan will be effective.

Annual Notice: Employers must provide employees with an annual notice at least 60 days before the start of the plan year that explains the employee's contribution options, employer contribution formula, and withdrawal rules.

Matching Contributions: Employers can choose to match employee contributions dollar-for-dollar up to 3% of the employee's salary, or make a non-elective contribution of 2% of the employee's salary.

Employee Deferrals: Employees can defer up to 100% of their compensation up to the annual limit into a Simple IRA.

Employee Catch-Up Contributions: Employees who are age 50 or older can make catch-up contributions up to an additional $3,000 per year.

Penalty-Free Withdrawals: Penalty-free withdrawals from a Simple IRA may be allowed for certain purposes, such as for the purchase of a first home or to pay for qualified education expenses.

Excess Contributions: Employers must monitor contributions to ensure that they do not exceed the annual limit. Excess contributions must be returned to the employee or corrected through a correction program.

Plan Termination: Employers may terminate a Simple IRA plan at any time, but may be subject to penalties and fees if the plan is terminated within two years of its inception.

Plan Disclosure: Employers must provide employees with an annual statement that includes the total contributions made to the employee's Simple IRA account for the year, the vesting schedule for any employer contributions, and the account balance at the end of the year.

Plan Compliance: Employers must comply with all IRS rules and regulations regarding Simple IRA plans, including annual reporting requirements and nondiscrimination testing.

Nondiscrimination Testing: Simple IRA plans are subject to certain nondiscrimination testing requirements that ensure the plan benefits all eligible employees, not just highly compensated employees.

Safe Harbor Provision: Employers can avoid the nondiscrimination testing requirements by adopting a "safe harbor" provision that requires the employer to make a 3% contribution to all eligible employees, regardless of whether they make employee contributions.

Employer Contributions: Employer contributions to a Simple IRA are tax-deductible as a business expense.

Employee Benefits: Employees benefit from a Simple IRA by having a tax-deferred savings vehicle that helps them save for retirement.

Employee Retirement Income Security Act (ERISA): Employers who offer a Simple IRA plan are subject to ERISA regulations, which require them to act in the best interests of plan participants, disclose plan information to participants, and follow certain fiduciary standards.

In conclusion, a Simple IRA can be a valuable retirement savings option for employees of small businesses. With the ability to make tax-deductible contributions and the potential for employer contributions, a Simple IRA can help employees save for retirement while reducing their tax burden. However, employers must follow IRS rules and regulations, provide employees with adequate information about the plan, and monitor contributions to ensure compliance with annual limits. Employees should also understand the plan's features, contribution limits, and withdrawal rules before deciding to participate in a Simple IRA.

How to Maximize Your Simple IRA Savings:

If you have a Simple IRA, there are several strategies you can use to maximize your retirement savings. Here are some tips to help you get the most out of your Simple IRA:

Take advantage of employer matching contributions: If your employer offers matching contributions, make sure to contribute enough to your Simple IRA to receive the maximum match.

Contribute as much as you can: For 2023, the contribution limit for Simple IRAs is $14,000, or $16,500 if you are age 50 or older. Make sure to contribute as much as you can afford to maximize your savings.

Automate your contributions: Set up automatic contributions to your Simple IRA to make sure you are consistently saving for retirement.

Increase your contributions over time: As you earn more and your expenses decrease, consider increasing your Simple IRA contributions to maximize your savings.

Make catch-up contributions: If you are age 50 or older, you can make catch-up contributions to your Simple IRA to maximize your savings.

Invest wisely: Choose investment options that align with your retirement goals and risk tolerance to maximize your returns.

Diversify your investments: Diversify your Simple IRA investments across multiple asset classes, such as stocks, bonds, and cash, to minimize risk.

Rebalance your portfolio regularly: Rebalance your Simple IRA portfolio regularly to ensure it remains aligned with your investment goals and risk tolerance.

Minimize fees and expenses: Choose Simple IRA investments with low fees and expenses to maximize your returns.

Consider a Roth IRA conversion: If you anticipate being in a higher tax bracket in retirement, consider converting your Simple IRA to a Roth IRA to maximize tax-free withdrawals.

Coordinate your Simple IRA contributions with other retirement accounts: Make sure to coordinate your Simple IRA contributions with other retirement accounts, such as a 401(k), to maximize your overall retirement savings.

Avoid early withdrawals: Avoid withdrawing funds from your Simple IRA before age 59 ½ to avoid penalties and taxes.

Consider a self-directed Simple IRA: If you have experience with alternative investments, such as real estate or private equity, consider a self-directed Simple IRA to maximize your investment options.

Take advantage of the tax deduction: Simple IRA contributions are tax-deductible, so make sure to take advantage of this benefit to reduce your taxable income.

Maximize compound interest: Maximize your Simple IRA savings by taking advantage of compound interest over time.

Consider a Simple IRA loan: If you need to borrow money, consider a Simple IRA loan, which allows you to borrow up to $50,000 or 50% of your account balance, whichever is less.

Plan for required minimum distributions: Keep in mind that you are required to take minimum distributions from your Simple IRA starting at age 72. Plan for these distributions to avoid penalties and taxes.

Think about your long-term retirement goals: Consider your long-term retirement goals and adjust your Simple IRA contributions and investments accordingly.

Keep track of your Simple IRA balance: Keep track of your Simple IRA balance to ensure you are on track to meet your retirement goals.

Review your Simple IRA annually: Review your Simple IRA annually to ensure it remains aligned with your retirement goals and risk tolerance.

Consider your estate planning needs: If you plan to leave your Simple IRA to your heirs, make sure to consider the impact of taxes and penalties on their inheritance.

Think about your health care costs: Consider your anticipated health care costs in retirement and adjust your Simple IRA contributions and investments accordingly.

Consider a financial advisor: Consider working with a financial advisor who can help you maximize your Simple IRA savings and develop a comprehensive retirement plan.

Keep your beneficiary designation up-to-date: Make sure to update your Simple IRA beneficiary designation regularly to ensure your assets are distributed according to your wishes.

Take advantage of education opportunities: Many financial institutions and retirement plan providers offer education opportunities to help you maximize your Simple IRA savings. Take advantage of these resources to learn more about retirement planning and investment strategies.

Be patient and stay the course: Saving for retirement takes time and patience. Stay the course and continue to make contributions to your Simple IRA to maximize your savings over time.

In conclusion, maximizing your Simple IRA savings requires careful planning, investment strategy, and patience. Take advantage of employer matching contributions, contribute as much as you can, automate your contributions, and invest wisely. Diversify your investments, minimize fees and expenses, consider a Roth IRA conversion, and coordinate your contributions with other retirement accounts. Avoid early withdrawals, plan for required minimum distributions, and consider your long-term retirement goals. Work with a financial advisor and take advantage of education opportunities to learn more about retirement planning and investment strategies. Most importantly, be patient and stay the course to maximize your Simple IRA savings over time.

Understanding 403(b) Plans:

A 403(b) plan is a type of retirement plan that is available to employees of certain tax-exempt organizations, such as schools, hospitals, and non-profit organizations. Here are some key things to understand about 403(b) plans:

Contributions are made on a pre-tax basis: Like a traditional 401(k) plan, contributions to a 403(b) plan are made on a pre-tax basis, which means they are deducted from your paycheck before taxes are applied.

Contributions are limited: For 2023, the contribution limit for a 403(b) plan is $19,500, or $26,000 if you are age 50 or older.

Catch-up contributions are available: If you are age 50 or older, you can make catch-up contributions to a 403(b) plan, which allows you to contribute more than the regular contribution limit.

Employer contributions may be available: Some employers may offer matching contributions to their employees' 403(b) plans, which can help increase your retirement savings.

Distributions are subject to income tax: Like other types of retirement plans, distributions from a 403(b) plan are subject to income tax.

Early withdrawals may be subject to penalties: If you withdraw money from a 403(b) plan before age 59 ½, you may be subject to a 10% penalty in addition to income tax.

Required minimum distributions are required: Once you reach age 72, you are required to take minimum distributions from your 403(b) plan each year.

Investment options may be limited: Unlike a 401(k) plan, which may offer a wide range of investment options, 403(b) plans may have limited investment options.

Plan fees may apply: Like other types of retirement plans, 403(b) plans may have fees associated with them, such as administrative fees and investment fees.

You may be able to transfer your plan: If you change employers or retire, you may be able to transfer your 403(b) plan to another retirement plan, such as an IRA or a new employer's retirement plan.

The plan is designed for non-profit organizations: 403(b) plans are designed specifically for employees of certain tax-exempt organizations, such as schools, hospitals, and non-profit organizations.

There may be restrictions on withdrawals: Depending on your plan, there may be restrictions on when and how you can withdraw money from your 403(b) plan.

The plan is subject to IRS rules: Like other types of retirement plans, 403(b) plans are subject to IRS rules and regulations.

The plan may offer loans: Some 403(b) plans may offer loans to participants, which allows you to borrow money from your retirement savings and pay it back over time.

The plan may offer a Roth option: Some 403(b) plans may offer a Roth option, which allows you to make after-tax contributions to your retirement savings.

The plan may offer a non-elective contribution option: Some employers may offer a non-elective contribution option, which means they will make contributions to your 403(b) plan regardless of whether you make contributions.

The plan may offer a profit-sharing option: Some employers may offer a profit-sharing option, which means they will make contributions to your 403(b) plan based on the profits of the organization.

You may be able to rollover other retirement accounts: If you have other retirement accounts, such as a traditional IRA or a 401(k) plan, you may be able to rollover those accounts into your 403(b) plan.

The plan may have vesting requirements: Depending on your plan, there may be vesting requirements, which means you may need to work for a certain period of time before you are fully entitled to your employer's contributions.

The plan may offer tax benefits: Contributing to a 403(b) plan can provide tax benefits, such as reducing your taxable income and potentially lowering your tax liability.

The plan may offer retirement income options: Some 403(b) plans may offer retirement income options, such as annuities or installment payments, which can provide a steady stream of income in retirement.

The plan may have a Roth conversion option: Some 403(b) plans may offer a Roth conversion option, which allows you to convert pre-tax contributions to after-tax Roth contributions.

The plan may allow for additional contributions: Some 403(b) plans may allow for additional contributions, such as after-tax contributions or employer profit-sharing contributions.

The plan may have a vesting schedule: Depending on your plan, your employer's contributions may be subject to a vesting schedule, which means you may only be entitled to a portion of their contributions based on the length of your employment.

The plan may have a limit on contributions: In addition to the annual contribution limit, some 403(b) plans may have a limit on the total amount of contributions that can be made.

Consult with a financial advisor: As with any retirement plan, it is important to consult with a financial advisor who can help you understand the specific features and benefits of your 403(b) plan and create a retirement savings strategy that meets your needs and goals.

How to Maximize Your 403(b) Savings:

A 403(b) plan is a type of retirement savings plan available to employees of certain nonprofit organizations, such as schools, hospitals, and churches. Here are some tips to help you maximize your 403(b) savings:

Start early: The earlier you start contributing to your 403(b) plan, the more time your money has to grow. Even small contributions made early on can have a big impact over time.

Contribute as much as possible: The more you can contribute to your 403(b) plan, the more you'll have saved for retirement. For 2023, the maximum contribution limit is $19,500, or $26,000 if you are age 50 or older.

Take advantage of employer matching: If your employer offers a matching contribution, make sure to contribute enough to take full advantage of the match. This is essentially free money that can boost your savings.

Consider a Roth 403(b) option: Some employers offer a Roth 403(b) option, which allows you to contribute after-tax dollars to your retirement savings. This can be a good option if you expect to be in a higher tax bracket in retirement.

Re-evaluate your contributions each year: Make sure to re-evaluate your contributions each year to ensure you are on track to meet your retirement savings goals. If you receive a raise or a bonus, consider increasing your contributions.

Take advantage of catch-up contributions: If you are age 50 or older, you can make catch-up contributions to your 403(b) plan. This can help you save even more for retirement.

Choose low-cost investment options: Make sure to choose low-cost investment options, such as index funds or exchange-traded funds (ETFs), to minimize fees and expenses and maximize your returns.

Diversify your investments: Diversification is key to managing risk in your portfolio. Make sure to diversify your investments across different asset classes, such as stocks, bonds, and real estate.

Consider a target-date fund: A target-date fund can be a good option if you are unsure how to allocate your investments. These funds automatically adjust the allocation of investments based on your expected retirement date.

Rebalance your portfolio regularly: Make sure to rebalance your portfolio regularly to ensure your investments are aligned with your goals and risk tolerance.

Review your plan's fees and expenses: Make sure to review your plan's fees and expenses to ensure you are not paying more than necessary. Look for low-cost investment options and consider investing in your plan's lowest-cost index funds.

Monitor your account performance: Keep track of how your account is performing and make adjustments as necessary to stay on track with your retirement savings goals.

Consider a financial advisor: If you are unsure how to manage your 403(b) investments or need help developing a retirement savings strategy, consider working with a financial advisor.

Think about your retirement timeline: Consider your retirement timeline when deciding how to allocate your investments. If you have a long time horizon before retirement, you may be able to take on more risk for potentially higher returns.

Look at your overall financial situation: Consider your overall financial situation, including your income, expenses, and debt, to determine how much you can afford to contribute to your 403(b) plan.

Think about your other retirement savings options: Make sure to consider other retirement savings options, such as individual retirement accounts (IRAs), to diversify your retirement savings.

Think about your risk tolerance: Consider your risk tolerance and how it aligns with your retirement savings goals. If you are risk-averse, you may want to consider more conservative investments.

Consider inflation: Keep in mind the impact of inflation on your retirement savings and consider investments that can help protect your savings from inflation.

Take advantage of educational resources: Many 403(b) plans offer educational resources, such as online tools, calculators, and retirement planning seminars, to help you make informed decisions about your retirement savings.

Keep your beneficiaries up to date: Make sure to keep your beneficiaries up to date on your 403(b) plan, as this will ensure that your retirement savings are distributed according to your wishes in the event of your death.

Consider your tax situation: Consider your current and future tax situation when deciding how much to contribute to your 403(b) plan. Contributions to a traditional 403(b) plan are tax-deductible, while withdrawals in retirement are taxed as income. Contributions to a Roth 403(b) plan are made with after-tax dollars, but withdrawals in retirement are tax-free.

Avoid early withdrawals: Try to avoid early withdrawals from your 403(b) plan, as these withdrawals are subject to income tax and a 10% penalty. Consider setting up an emergency fund to cover unexpected expenses instead.

Don't forget about required minimum distributions: Once you reach age 72, you will be required to take minimum distributions from your 403(b) plan each year. Make sure to factor this into your retirement planning.

Stay informed about plan changes: Keep yourself informed about any changes to your 403(b) plan, such as changes to investment options or fees and expenses. This will help you make informed decisions about your retirement savings.

Consider your estate planning needs: If you have significant assets in your 403(b) plan, make sure to consider your estate planning needs. Work with a financial advisor or estate planning attorney to develop a plan that will help protect your assets and ensure they are distributed according to your wishes.

Keep your retirement savings goals in mind: Ultimately, the key to maximizing your 403(b) savings is to keep your retirement savings goals in mind and make decisions that align with those goals. Regularly review your progress and make adjustments as necessary to ensure you stay on track to achieve the retirement you envision.

Understanding Defined Benefit Plans

A defined benefit plan is a type of retirement plan in which an employer promises to pay a specific amount of retirement income to an employee upon retirement. The amount of retirement income is based on a formula that typically takes into account the employee's salary, years of service, and age at retirement.

Defined benefit plans are usually funded by the employer, although some plans may require employee contributions as well. The employer contributes funds to the plan over time, and these funds are invested to generate returns that will be used to pay retirement benefits to employees.

Defined benefit plans are generally considered to be more advantageous than other types of retirement plans, such as defined contribution plans like 401(k)s, because they offer a guaranteed income stream in retirement.

The amount of retirement income promised by a defined benefit plan is typically expressed as a percentage of the employee's salary at retirement. For example, a plan may promise to pay an employee 2% of their final average salary for every year of service.

In order to be eligible for a defined benefit plan, an employee usually needs to work for the employer for a certain number of years, known as a vesting period. Once an employee has met the vesting requirements, they are entitled to receive the promised retirement benefits even if they leave the employer before retirement.

Defined benefit plans are generally considered to be more advantageous for employees who plan to work for an employer for a long period of time, since the amount of retirement benefits is typically based on years of service.

However, defined benefit plans may be less advantageous for employees who plan to change employers frequently or who have irregular work patterns, since they may not meet the vesting requirements for the plan.

One advantage of defined benefit plans for employers is that they can help to attract and retain talented employees. Employees may be more likely to stay with an employer that offers a generous retirement plan.

Defined benefit plans also allow employers to control the investment strategy of the plan, since they are responsible for investing the funds in the plan. This can allow employers to manage the risk of the plan more effectively.

One disadvantage of defined benefit plans for employers is that they can be expensive to fund, especially if the plan promises generous retirement benefits. Employers must contribute funds to the plan regularly to ensure that there is enough money to pay retirement benefits to employees.

Employers may also be required to purchase annuities or other insurance products to protect the plan against investment risk or longevity risk, which can add to the cost of the plan.

Defined benefit plans are also subject to complex regulatory requirements, which can make them more difficult and expensive to administer than other types of retirement plans.

One potential disadvantage of defined benefit plans for employees is that they may not have as much control over their retirement savings as they would with a defined contribution plan like a 401(k). With a defined benefit plan, the employer is responsible for investing the funds in the plan, and employees may not have as much say in the investment strategy.

Defined benefit plans may also be less portable than other types of retirement plans, since employees may need to meet vesting requirements and work for an employer for a certain number of years to be eligible for retirement benefits.

One advantage of defined benefit plans for retirees is that they offer a guaranteed income stream in retirement. This can provide retirees with greater financial security and stability.

Defined benefit plans also provide retirees with protection against inflation, since the retirement benefits are typically adjusted for inflation over time.

However, one potential disadvantage of defined benefit plans for retirees is that they may not have as much control over their retirement savings as they would with a defined contribution plan. With a defined benefit plan, retirees are typically locked into the promised retirement benefits and may not be able to make changes to their investment strategy.

Defined benefit plans may also be subject to funding challenges, especially if investment returns are lower than expected or if the plan's liabilities are greater than expected due to changes in the workforce or other factors.

If a defined benefit plan becomes underfunded, the employer may be required to make additional contributions to the plan to ensure that there is enough money to pay retirement benefits to employees.

Defined benefit plans are also subject to regulations that require employers to report on the financial health of the plan and take steps to ensure that the plan remains financially stable over time.

One potential advantage of defined benefit plans for retirees is that they may be eligible for additional benefits, such as survivor benefits or disability benefits. These benefits can provide additional financial protection to retirees and their families.

Defined benefit plans may also offer retirees the option to receive retirement benefits in the form of a lump sum payment, which can provide greater flexibility and control over retirement savings.
However, retirees should carefully consider the risks and benefits of taking a lump sum payment, since they may be giving up the security of a guaranteed income stream in retirement.

Overall, defined benefit plans can offer significant advantages to both employers and employees, including a guaranteed income stream in retirement and greater financial security and stability.

However, defined benefit plans are subject to complex regulatory requirements and can be expensive to fund and administer, which may make them less appealing to some employers.

Employees should carefully consider their retirement goals and work patterns when deciding whether a defined benefit plan is right for them, while employers should carefully evaluate the costs and benefits of offering a defined benefit plan to their employees.

Ultimately, the decision to offer or participate in a defined benefit plan should be based on a careful evaluation of the risks and benefits of the plan and the unique needs and circumstances of the employer and employees involved.

How to Maximize Your Defined Benefit Plan Benefits:

Maximizing your defined benefit plan benefits is an important part of planning for your retirement. Here are some tips to help you make the most of your defined benefit plan:

Understand your plan: The first step in maximizing your defined benefit plan benefits is to understand the plan itself. Read through the plan documents carefully, paying special attention to the benefit calculation formula, vesting requirements, and any early retirement options.

Stay with your employer for the long-term: Defined benefit plans are designed to reward employees who stay with their employer for the long-term. If you switch jobs frequently, you may not be able to accumulate enough years of service to qualify for a significant benefit.

Maximize your years of service: Your defined benefit plan benefit is calculated based on your years of service with your employer. Maximize your benefit by staying with your employer for as long as possible and working full-time.

Consider your retirement age: Your defined benefit plan benefit may be higher if you wait until your full retirement age to retire. Consider delaying retirement if possible to maximize your benefit.

Understand your benefit calculation formula: Your defined benefit plan benefit is typically calculated based on a formula that takes into account your years of service and your final average pay. Make sure you understand how the formula works so you can make informed decisions about your retirement timing.

Maximize your final average pay: Your final average pay is a key factor in your defined benefit plan benefit calculation. Maximize your final average pay by working full-time, taking advantage of any salary increases or promotions, and avoiding any periods of reduced pay.

Take advantage of any catch-up contributions: Some defined benefit plans allow catch-up contributions for employees who are close to retirement age. Consider taking advantage of these contributions if available to boost your benefit.

Consider your spouse's benefit: Many defined benefit plans offer survivor benefits for spouses. Consider how your retirement timing and benefit election may impact your spouse's benefit.

Understand your vesting schedule: Your defined benefit plan may have a vesting schedule that determines how much of the benefit you are entitled to if you leave your employer before retirement age. Make sure you understand the vesting schedule and its impact on your benefit.

Consider any early retirement options: Your defined benefit plan may offer early retirement options, such as reduced benefits for retiring before your full retirement age. Consider whether these options are right for you based on your financial needs and retirement goals.

Consider any inflation protection options: Some defined benefit plans offer inflation protection options, such as cost-of-living adjustments (COLAs). Consider whether these options are right for you based on your retirement goals and financial needs.

Keep track of your benefit statements: Make sure to review your defined benefit plan benefit statements regularly to ensure they are accurate and up-to-date. Notify your employer of any discrepancies or errors.

Consider your other retirement accounts: Your defined benefit plan is just one part of your overall retirement strategy. Consider how your other retirement accounts, such as a 401(k) or IRA, may impact your retirement income and benefit needs.

Plan for taxes: Your defined benefit plan benefit may be subject to income taxes in retirement. Plan for these taxes as part of your overall retirement planning strategy.

Consider any required minimum distributions: If you have other retirement accounts in addition to your defined benefit plan, you may be subject to required minimum distributions (RMDs) in retirement. Make sure to plan for these distributions as part of your retirement income needs.

Review your beneficiary designations: Make sure your beneficiary designations are up-to-date and accurately reflect your wishes. Keep in mind that your beneficiary designation can impact your spouse's survivor benefit.

Understand your lump sum payout options: Some defined benefit plans offer a lump sum payout option instead of a monthly annuity. Make sure you understand the pros and cons of each option and how they may impact your retirement income.

Consider any early retirement subsidies: Some defined benefit plans offer early retirement subsidies, which provide a higher benefit for retiring before your full retirement age. Consider whether these subsidies are right for you based on your financial needs and retirement goals.

Plan for healthcare costs: Healthcare costs can be a significant expense in retirement. Make sure to plan for these costs as part of your overall retirement planning strategy, including any healthcare benefits provided by your defined benefit plan.

Seek professional advice: Maximizing your defined benefit plan benefits can be complex and may require professional advice. Consider consulting with a financial planner or retirement specialist to help you make informed decisions about your retirement income and benefit needs.

In summary, maximizing your defined benefit plan benefits requires careful planning and understanding of the plan itself. By staying with your employer for the long-term, maximizing your years of service and final average pay, understanding the benefit calculation formula, and considering your retirement age, you can help ensure that you receive the maximum benefit possible. Additionally, considering early retirement options, inflation protection options, and healthcare costs, as well as seeking professional advice, can help you make informed decisions about your retirement income and benefit needs.

Understanding Social Security:

Social Security is a federal program that provides financial assistance to people who have reached retirement age, as well as to people with disabilities, and to the survivors of people who have died. Here are some important things to understand about Social Security:

⬜ Eligibility: To be eligible for Social Security retirement benefits, you must have earned at least 40 Social Security credits through your work history, which generally means working for at least 10 years.

⬜ Retirement age: The full retirement age for Social Security benefits varies depending on the year you were born. For people born in 1960 or later, the full retirement age is 67.

⬜ Early retirement: You can start receiving Social Security retirement benefits as early as age 62, but your benefit amount will be reduced if you start before your full retirement age.

⬜ Delayed retirement: If you delay starting Social Security retirement benefits beyond your full retirement age, your benefit amount will increase by a certain percentage each year, up to age 70.

⬜ Spousal benefits: If you are married, you may be eligible for spousal benefits based on your spouse's work history, even if you have never worked or paid into Social Security.

⬜ Survivor benefits: If your spouse or parent dies, you may be eligible for survivor benefits based on their work history.

⬜ Disability benefits: If you are disabled and unable to work, you may be eligible for Social Security disability benefits.

⬜ Benefit amount: Your Social Security retirement benefit amount is based on your highest 35 years of earnings, adjusted for inflation. The formula used to calculate your benefit amount is complex, so it's important to review your Social Security statement to understand your estimated benefit amount.

⬜ Income taxes: Depending on your income, a portion of your Social Security benefits may be subject to federal income tax.

⬜ Cost-of-living adjustments: Social Security benefits are adjusted each year to account for inflation, based on the Consumer Price Index for Urban Wage Earners and Clerical Workers (CPI-W).

⬜ Medicare: If you are eligible for Social Security retirement benefits, you are also eligible for Medicare, which provides health insurance coverage for people age 65 and older.

⬜ Social Security trust funds: Social Security is funded through payroll taxes paid by workers and their employers. The funds are held in two trust funds, the Old-Age and Survivors Insurance (OASI) trust fund and the Disability Insurance (DI) trust fund.

⬜ Financial stability: The Social Security trust funds are projected to become insolvent in the coming decades, which means that the program may not be able to pay full benefits to all eligible recipients. Various proposals have been made to address this issue, including raising taxes, reducing benefits, or both.

▒   Retirement savings: Social Security is intended to be one part of your overall retirement income. It's important to also save for retirement through other means, such as a 401(k) or IRA.

▒   Benefit estimates: You can estimate your Social Security retirement benefit amount using the Social Security Administration's online calculator or by reviewing your Social Security statement.

▒   Filing for benefits: You can file for Social Security retirement benefits online, by phone, or in person at a Social Security office.

▒   Working while receiving benefits: If you start receiving Social Security retirement benefits before your full retirement age and continue to work, your benefit amount may be reduced if you earn more than a certain amount each year.

▒   Taxation of benefits: If your income exceeds certain thresholds, a portion of your Social Security benefits may be subject to federal income tax.

▒   Social Security scams: Be aware of Social Security scams, where scammers try to get you to provide personal information or make payments by claiming to be from the Social Security Administration.

▒   Appeals process: If your Social Security benefits application is denied, you have the right to appeal the decision. The appeals process can be complex, so it's important to consult with an attorney or other expert.

Overall, understanding Social Security is an important part of planning for retirement and financial stability. Knowing your eligibility, benefit amount, and options for filing can help you make the most of the program, while also considering other retirement savings strategies. Keeping up to date on changes to the program and potential reforms can also help you plan for the future and ensure financial security in retirement.

How to Maximize Your Social Security Benefits:

Social Security benefits are an essential source of retirement income for millions of Americans. Here are some tips to help you maximize your Social Security benefits:

Work at least 35 years: Social Security benefits are based on your highest 35 years of earnings. If you have worked fewer than 35 years, zeros are factored into the calculation, which can significantly reduce your benefit amount.

Delay claiming benefits: You can start claiming Social Security benefits as early as age 62, but if you delay claiming until your full retirement age (between 66 and 67, depending on your birth year), your benefit amount will increase by 8% per year until age 70.

Consider working longer: Working longer can increase your Social Security benefits in two ways. First, it allows you to replace low-earning years in the benefit calculation with higher-earning years. Second, it allows you to delay claiming benefits, which can increase your benefit amount.

Optimize your earnings record: Make sure that your earnings record is accurate and up-to-date. Errors in your earnings record can result in lower Social Security benefits.

Coordinate with your spouse: If you are married, coordinating your Social Security claiming strategy with your spouse can help you maximize your benefits. Strategies may include claiming spousal benefits or delaying claiming to increase your benefit amount.

Claim spousal benefits: If you are married and your spouse has a higher Social Security benefit, you may be eligible for spousal benefits. You can claim spousal benefits as early as age 62, but your benefit amount will be reduced.

Consider survivor benefits: If you are married, your spouse may be eligible for survivor benefits if you die first. Maximizing your own Social Security benefits can help ensure that your spouse has a secure retirement income.

Coordinate with other retirement income: Coordinate your Social Security claiming strategy with other sources of retirement income, such as pensions or 401(k) plans, to maximize your overall retirement income.

Consider your health: If you are in good health and expect to live a long time, delaying claiming Social Security benefits may be a good strategy since your benefit amount will increase over time.

Understand the impact of working: If you claim Social Security benefits before your full retirement age and continue working, your benefits may be reduced if you earn more than a certain amount.

Factor in taxes: Social Security benefits are subject to federal income taxes if your income exceeds a certain threshold. Factor in the impact of taxes when deciding when to claim benefits.

Take advantage of claiming strategies: There are several claiming strategies, such as file and suspend and restricted application, that can help you maximize your Social Security benefits. Make sure to explore all of your options.

Look at the impact of inflation: Social Security benefits are adjusted for inflation each year, but inflation can erode the value of your benefits over time. Factor in the impact of inflation when deciding when to claim benefits.

Consider your overall retirement income needs: Consider your overall retirement income needs and how Social Security benefits fit into your retirement income strategy.

Understand the impact of divorce: If you are divorced, you may be eligible for Social Security benefits based on your ex-spouse's earnings record. Make sure to explore all of your options.

Look at the impact of disability: If you become disabled before reaching retirement age, you may be eligible for Social Security disability benefits. Make sure to explore all of your options.

Understand the impact of remarriage: If you remarry after age 60, you may be eligible for survivor benefits based on your former spouse's earnings record. Make sure to explore all of your options.

Plan for unexpected expenses: Social Security benefits may not be enough to cover all of your retirement expenses. Plan for unexpected expenses, such as medical bills or home repairs, to ensure that you have enough retirement income.

Stay informed about changes to Social Security: Social Security rules and regulations can change over time. Stay informed about changes that may impact your benefits and adjust your retirement income strategy accordingly.

Seek professional advice: Maximizing your Social Security benefits can be complex. Seek professional advice from a financial advisor or Social Security expert to ensure that you are making the best decisions for your retirement income strategy. They can help you navigate the various claiming strategies, coordinate with other sources of retirement income, and factor in your unique circumstances to help you maximize your Social Security benefits.

Understanding Required Minimum Distributions (RMDs):

Required Minimum Distributions (RMDs) are a critical aspect of retirement planning. They are the minimum amount you must withdraw from certain retirement accounts each year once you reach a certain age. Here are some key things to understand about RMDs:

What accounts are subject to RMDs: RMDs apply to traditional IRAs, SEP IRAs, SIMPLE IRAs, 401(k)s, 403(b)s, and other types of defined contribution plans.

When RMDs start: RMDs must begin by April 1 of the year following the year you turn 72, or 70½ if you reached that age before January 1, 2020.

How RMDs are calculated: RMDs are calculated based on your account balance and life expectancy. The IRS provides life expectancy tables to help calculate the required distribution.

What happens if you don't take your RMD: If you do not take your RMD, you may be subject to a penalty equal to 50% of the amount you were supposed to withdraw.

How RMDs are taxed: RMDs are taxed as ordinary income in the year they are withdrawn.

How RMDs impact your taxes: RMDs can increase your taxable income, which can impact your tax rate and eligibility for certain tax credits and deductions.

Strategies for managing RMDs: Some strategies for managing RMDs include converting traditional IRA assets to a Roth IRA, making charitable contributions from your IRA, and using the RMD to purchase a qualified longevity annuity contract (QLAC).

What happens if you inherit an account subject to RMDs: If you inherit an account subject to RMDs, you may be required to take distributions based on your own life expectancy or a set schedule.

How RMDs impact your retirement income: RMDs can impact your retirement income by reducing the amount of money you have in your retirement accounts and potentially increasing your tax liability.

Exceptions to RMDs: There are some exceptions to RMDs, such as for Roth IRAs and certain defined benefit plans.

How RMDs impact your asset allocation: RMDs can impact your asset allocation by reducing the amount of money you have in your retirement accounts and potentially changing your investment strategy.

What happens if you have multiple accounts subject to RMDs: If you have multiple accounts subject to RMDs, you can choose to take the distributions from any one or a combination of those accounts.

The impact of the SECURE Act on RMDs: The SECURE Act changed the age at which RMDs must start to 72, up from 70½.

The impact of the CARES Act on RMDs: The CARES Act waived RMDs for 2020 in response to the COVID-19 pandemic.

How RMDs impact your estate planning: RMDs can impact your estate planning by reducing the amount of money you have in your retirement accounts and potentially changing your inheritance plan.

What happens if you have a spouse who is more than 10 years younger: If you have a spouse who is more than 10 years younger, you may be able to use a joint life expectancy table to calculate your RMDs, which can result in lower distributions.

The impact of inflation on RMDs: Inflation can impact RMDs by reducing the purchasing power of the required distribution over time.

How RMDs impact your withdrawal strategy: RMDs can impact your withdrawal strategy by requiring you to withdraw a certain amount each year, which can impact your tax liability and income needs.

The impact of market volatility on RMDs: Market volatility can impact RMDs by causing fluctuations in the value of your retirement accounts, which can impact the amount of money you need to withdraw to meet the minimum distribution requirement.

The importance of planning for RMDs: Planning for RMDs is important to ensure you have enough retirement income, minimize your tax liability, and avoid penalties for failing to take the required distributions. It is important to work with a financial advisor to develop a plan that meets your individual needs and goals.

In summary, understanding RMDs is essential for successful retirement planning. RMDs are minimum distributions required from certain retirement accounts once you reach a certain age. They are calculated based on your account balance and life expectancy and can impact your taxes, retirement income, and investment strategy. There are strategies for managing RMDs, such as converting traditional IRA assets to a Roth IRA or making charitable contributions from your IRA. It is important to plan for RMDs to ensure you have enough retirement income, minimize your tax liability, and avoid penalties for failing to take the required distributions. Work with a financial advisor to develop a plan that meets your individual needs and goals.

How to Manage Your RMDs:

RMDs, or Required Minimum Distributions, are withdrawals that the IRS requires you to take from your retirement accounts starting at age 72 (or age 70 ½ if you were born before July 1, 1949). Here are some tips for managing your RMDs:

a. Know when your RMDs are due: RMDs must be taken by December 31 of each year, starting in the year you turn age 72 (or age 70 ½ if you were born before July 1, 1949).

b. Understand the penalty for not taking your RMDs: If you fail to take your RMDs on time, you could face a penalty of up to 50% of the amount you were supposed to withdraw.

c. Calculate your RMD amount: Your RMD amount is calculated based on the balance of your retirement accounts and your life expectancy, so make sure to use the correct formula to calculate your RMD amount.

d. Consider consolidating your retirement accounts: If you have multiple retirement accounts, consider consolidating them to make it easier to manage your RMDs.

e. Plan for your tax liability: Remember that RMDs are taxable income, so plan for the tax liability that comes with taking RMDs.

f. Consider using RMDs for charitable giving: If you are charitably inclined, consider using your RMDs to make charitable donations and reduce your tax liability.

g. Consider delaying your RMDs if you are still working: If you are still working and do not need to take your RMDs to cover your living expenses, you may be able to delay taking your RMDs until you retire.

h. Plan for the impact of RMDs on your overall retirement income: Remember that RMDs will impact your overall retirement income, so make sure to plan accordingly.

i. Consider using a Qualified Charitable Distribution (QCD): A QCD allows you to donate your RMDs directly to a qualified charity, which can help reduce your tax liability.

j. Review your beneficiary designations: Make sure your beneficiary designations are up -to-date and reflect your current wishes.

k. Consider using a professional financial planner: A professional financial planner can help you manage your RMDs and make the best decisions for your retirement.

l. Think about using a partial RMD strategy: If you have multiple retirement accounts, you may be able to take a partial RMD from one account and leave the rest untouched.

m. Consider using RMDs to cover your living expenses: If you need the money, you can use your RMDs to cover your living expenses, but remember to plan for the tax liability.

n. Review your investment strategy: Review your investment strategy and make sure it aligns with your RMD needs.

o. Consider the impact of RMDs on your Social Security benefits: Remember that RMDs can impact your Social Security benefits, so make sure to plan accordingly.

p. Think about using a Roth conversion: If you anticipate being in a higher tax bracket in the future, consider converting some of your Traditional IRA assets to a Roth IRA to reduce your future RMDs.

q. Consider using a qualified longevity annuity contract (QLAC): A QLAC allows you to use a portion of your retirement savings to purchase an annuity that starts at a later age, which can help reduce your RMDs.

r. Plan for the impact of RMDs on your estate planning: RMDs can impact your estate planning, so make sure to review your plan and make any necessary adjustments.

s. Consider using a distribution plan: A distribution plan can help you manage your RMDs and ensure that you take the correct amount each year.

t. Stay informed: Keep yourself informed about any changes to RMD rules or regulations that may affect you, and be proactive in making any necessary adjustments to your retirement planning.

u. Understand the impact of RMDs on your retirement lifestyle: Remember that RMDs will impact your overall retirement lifestyle, so make sure to plan accordingly and adjust your expectations as necessary.

v. Don't forget about your IRA contributions: While RMDs require you to take money out of your retirement accounts, don't forget about the importance of continuing to make IRA contributions to ensure you have enough saved for retirement.

w. Consider using a financial advisor: A financial advisor can help you manage your RMDs and ensure that you are making the best decisions for your retirement.

x. Think about the impact of RMDs on your legacy: RMDs can impact your legacy planning, so make sure to review your plan and make any necessary adjustments.

y. Remember the importance of diversification: Diversification is key to a successful retirement plan, so make sure to diversify your retirement savings across different types of accounts and investment vehicles.

z. Be flexible: Retirement planning is a dynamic process, so be flexible and willing to make adjustments as necessary to ensure that you are able to meet your financial goals.

In conclusion, managing RMDs can be a complex and challenging task, but with careful planning and consideration of your unique financial situation, you can effectively manage your RMDs and ensure that you are able to enjoy a comfortable retirement. Stay informed, work with a financial advisor, and be willing to make adjustments as necessary to stay on track toward achieving your retirement goals.

How to Choose the Right Retirement Account for Your Needs

The type of retirement account you choose will depend on several factors, including your age, income, and retirement goals.

If you're younger and have a long time horizon before retirement, a 401(k) or Roth IRA may be a good option.

If you're older and closer to retirement age, a traditional IRA or pension may be a better fit.

Consider your employer's retirement benefits when choosing a retirement account, as many employers offer matching contributions to 401(k) plans.

Research and compare the fees, expenses, and investment options of different retirement accounts before making a decision.

Strategies for Maximizing Your Retirement Savings

o   Start saving for retirement as early as possible, even if it's just a small amount each month.

o   Take advantage of employer-sponsored retirement plans, such as 401(k)s, and contribute enough to receive the full employer match.

o   Consider opening a Roth IRA, which allows you to contribute after-tax income and withdraw funds tax-free in retirement.

o   Increase your retirement contributions each year, as your income and expenses allow.

o   Avoid taking early withdrawals from retirement accounts, as they can incur taxes and penalties and reduce the amount of money you have available in retirement.

o   Another strategy for maximizing retirement savings is to invest in a diversified portfolio of stocks, bonds, and other assets.

o   Consider hiring a financial advisor to help you make investment decisions and create a retirement savings plan.

o   Consider delaying retirement, as working longer can provide additional time to save money and increase your retirement income.

o   If you have multiple retirement accounts, consolidate them into one account to simplify management and reduce fees.

o   Consider downsizing your home or reducing other expenses to free up additional money for retirement savings.

o   Take advantage of catch-up contributions if you're over 50 years old, as these allow you to contribute more to retirement accounts.

o   Consider a target-date fund, which is designed to automatically adjust the asset allocation of your retirement investments as you approach retirement age.

o   Avoid taking on too much debt, as this can reduce your ability to save for retirement.

o   Consider investing in real estate, either through rental properties or real estate investment trusts (REITs), to diversify your retirement portfolio.

o Regularly review your retirement savings plan and make adjustments as needed to stay on track to meet your goals.

o Plan for healthcare costs in retirement, as these can be a significant expense.

o Consider long-term care insurance to help cover the costs of medical care and assistance in later life.

o Consider working part-time or starting a small business in retirement to supplement your income.

o Prepare for unexpected events, such as a job loss or health issue, by having an emergency fund set aside.

o Finally, be patient and consistent with your retirement savings plan, and remember that small contributions and consistent investment can add up to a significant retirement fund over time.

Devon R. Blackwell

Chapter 7: Common Investment Mistakes to Avoid

Avoiding Emotional Investing: One of the most common investment mistakes is allowing emotions to drive investment decisions. When investors let fear, greed, or anxiety take over, they may make impulsive decisions that can hurt their portfolios in the long run. To avoid this, investors should create an investment plan and stick to it, no matter what the market is doing.

Staying Focused on Your Long-Term Goals: Another mistake that investors often make is losing sight of their long-term goals. They may become too focused on short-term market movements or hot trends, instead of staying committed to their investment plan. To stay on track, investors should regularly review their portfolio and make adjustments as necessary to ensure they are on course to achieve their long-term financial goals.

Diversification: A key principle of investing is diversification, or spreading your investments across a range of different asset classes, industries, and geographies. This helps to reduce risk and maximize returns over time. However, some investors make the mistake of putting too much money into a single stock or asset class, which can leave their portfolio vulnerable to market volatility.

Chasing Hot Stocks: Another common mistake is chasing hot stocks or trends, hoping to make a quick profit. However, this strategy can be risky, as hot stocks may be overvalued and could fall quickly. It's important to do your due diligence and invest in stocks with strong fundamentals and good long-term prospects.

Ignoring Fees: Many investors underestimate the impact of fees on their investment returns. High fees can eat away at your profits over time, so it's important to choose low-cost investment options and to be aware of any hidden fees or charges.

Market Timing: Trying to time the market is another mistake that many investors make. However, it's difficult to predict market movements, and trying to time the market can lead to missed opportunities and losses. Instead, investors should focus on creating a well-diversified portfolio and sticking to their investment plan.

Lack of Patience: Investing is a long-term game, and it's important to have patience and stick to your investment plan even during times of market volatility. Investors who panic and sell during market downturns may miss out on potential gains when the market recovers.

Failing to Rebalance: Another mistake that investors often make is failing to rebalance their portfolio regularly. Over time, different investments will perform differently, which can cause your portfolio to become unbalanced. Rebalancing involves selling some assets and buying others to bring your portfolio back into line with your target asset allocation.

Overconfidence: Overconfidence can be a dangerous trait for investors, as it can lead them to take on too much risk or make impulsive decisions based on incomplete information. It's important to remain humble and to rely on data and analysis when making investment decisions.

Not Doing Your Research: Investing requires a certain level of research and due diligence to identify the best investment opportunities. Investors who fail to do their research may miss out on valuable information and opportunities that could help them achieve their financial goals.

Following the Crowd: Following the crowd is another mistake that investors often make. Just because everyone else is investing in a particular stock or asset class doesn't mean it's the right choice for you. Investors should focus on their own investment plan and goals, rather than following the herd.

Holding Too Much Cash: Holding too much cash can be a mistake, as it can limit your potential returns over time. While it's important to have some cash on hand for emergencies, investors should consider investing their cash in low-risk options that offer some potential returns, such as high-yield savings accounts or short-term bond funds.

Overreacting to News: Investors who overreact to news and headlines can make poor investment decisions based on incomplete information. It's important to take a long-term perspective and to avoid making rash decisions based on short-term market movements or news events.

Lack of Discipline: Sticking to an investment plan requires discipline and self-control. Investors who lack discipline may make impulsive decisions based on emotions or short-term market movements, which can hurt their portfolio over time.

Focusing on Past Performance: Investors who focus too much on past performance may be tempted to chase after high-performing stocks or funds, which can be risky. Past performance is not a guarantee of future results, and investors should instead focus on factors such as a company's fundamentals, management team, and long-term growth prospects.

Trying to Beat the Market: Trying to beat the market is a common mistake that many investors make. However, it's difficult to consistently outperform the market over the long term, and attempting to do so can lead to unnecessary risk and volatility.

Failing to Take Advantage of Tax-Efficient Strategies: Taxes can have a significant impact on investment returns, and failing to take advantage of tax-efficient investment strategies can hurt your bottom line. Investors should consider options such as tax-deferred retirement accounts and tax-loss harvesting to minimize their tax burden and maximize their returns.

Not Having a Contingency Plan: Investors who fail to plan for unexpected events such as job loss or market downturns may find themselves in a difficult financial situation. It's important to have a contingency plan in place that includes an emergency fund, insurance coverage, and a flexible investment strategy.

Overestimating Your Risk Tolerance: Risk tolerance is a key factor in determining your investment strategy, and investors who overestimate their risk tolerance may be taking on too much risk. It's important to understand your own risk tolerance and to invest in a way that aligns with your comfort level.

Investing Without a Clear Strategy: Finally, one of the biggest mistakes that investors can make is investing without a clear strategy or plan. Investing requires a thoughtful approach that takes into account your financial goals, risk tolerance, and time horizon. Investors who lack a clear strategy may find themselves making haphazard investment decisions that don't align with their long-term goals.

Devon R. Blackwell

CONCLUSION

Recap of Key Concepts

Investing is an essential part of achieving your financial goals. Whether you want to save for retirement, buy a home, or build wealth, investing can help you reach your objectives. By investing your money, you give it the opportunity to grow over time and potentially earn a higher return than other savings options.

To get started with investing, you need to understand the basics of stocks and bonds. Stocks represent ownership in a company, while bonds are a form of debt that can be issued by companies or governments. Both stocks and bonds carry different risks and potential rewards, so it's important to choose investments that align with your goals and risk tolerance.

Asset allocation is a critical part of investing. This refers to the process of diversifying your portfolio across different asset classes, such as stocks, bonds, and cash. By diversifying your portfolio, you can potentially reduce your overall risk and increase your chances of achieving long-term growth.

Building a diversified portfolio requires careful consideration of your investment goals and risk tolerance. You may need to research different investments and evaluate their potential risks and returns. By spreading your investments across different asset classes and types of investments, you can reduce the impact of any one investment on your overall portfolio.

Investing for retirement is a crucial aspect of financial planning. Retirement accounts, such as 401(k)s and IRAs, can offer tax benefits and potential investment growth over time. It's important to choose the right type of retirement account for your needs and contribute as much as possible to maximize your savings.

Finally, it's important to avoid common investment mistakes, such as making emotional decisions based on market fluctuations or failing to stay focused on your long-term goals. By maintaining a disciplined approach to investing and staying informed about your investments, you can improve your chances of achieving financial success over time. Remember, investing is a long-term strategy, so don't get discouraged by short-term fluctuations in the market.

Next Steps for Your Investing Journey

After reading this beginner's guide to investing, you should feel more confident about navigating the world of stocks and bonds. However, investing is an ongoing process that requires continuous learning and adjustment. Here are some next steps you can take to continue your investing journey:

Develop an investing plan: Now that you have a basic understanding of investing, take some time to develop a personalized investing plan. This should include your long-term goals, your risk tolerance, and your investment timeline. By having a plan in place, you can stay focused on your goals and make informed investment decisions.

Keep learning: Investing is a complex and ever-changing field, so it's important to stay up-to-date on the latest trends and best practices. Consider reading books, attending seminars or webinars, or following reputable investing blogs to continue expanding your knowledge.

Consider hiring a financial advisor: If you feel overwhelmed by the prospect of investing or want some additional guidance, consider hiring a financial advisor. A professional advisor can help you develop a personalized investment plan, provide guidance on investment selection, and monitor your progress over time.

Monitor your investments: Once you've started investing, it's important to monitor your investments regularly to ensure they're performing as expected. Check in on your portfolio regularly and make adjustments as needed to ensure you're on track to meet your goals.

Avoid emotional investing: It's natural to feel emotional about your investments, particularly during times of market volatility. However, making investment decisions based on fear or greed can lead to poor outcomes. Instead, stay focused on your long-term goals and stick to your investing plan.

Stay disciplined: Investing requires discipline and patience. Avoid making impulsive decisions based on short-term market movements, and stay focused on your long-term goals. By remaining disciplined and patient, you can achieve your financial goals and build a solid foundation for your future. Remember that investing is a long-term game, and it's important to stay focused on your goals even during times of market turbulence.

In conclusion, investing can be a powerful tool for building wealth and achieving your financial goals. By following the tips and strategies outlined in this guide, you can begin your investing journey with confidence and make informed decisions that support your long-term success. Remember to stay disciplined, keep learning, and monitor your investments regularly to ensure you're on track to meet your goals. With time and dedication, you can build a diversified portfolio that supports your financial dreams and aspirations. Good luck on your investing journey!

APPENDIX: GLOSSARY OF KEY TERMS

o Asset allocation: The process of dividing your investments among different asset classes, such as stocks, bonds, and cash, to achieve a desired balance of risk and return.

o Bond: A debt security that represents a loan made by an investor to a borrower, typically a corporation or government entity.

o Brokerage: A company or individual that buys and sells securities on behalf of investors.

o Bull market: A market in which stock prices are rising and investor confidence is high.

o Capital gains: The profits earned from selling an investment for more than its purchase price.

o Diversification: The practice of spreading your investments across multiple asset classes, sectors, and individual securities to reduce risk.

o Dividend: A portion of a company's profits that is distributed to shareholders on a regular basis.

o Index fund: A mutual fund or exchange-traded fund (ETF) that tracks the performance of a particular market index, such as the S&P 500.

o Portfolio: A collection of investments, such as stocks, bonds, and mutual funds, held by an individual or organization.

o Risk tolerance: An individual's ability to tolerate fluctuations in the value of their investments without selling them.

o Stock: A share in the ownership of a company that represents a claim on part of the company's assets and earnings.

o Stock exchange: A marketplace where stocks and other securities are traded among investors.

o Stock market index: A measure of the performance of a particular segment of the stock market, such as the Dow Jones Industrial Average or the Nasdaq Composite.

o Volatility: The degree to which the price of a security or market index fluctuates over time.

o Yield: The income earned from an investment, typically expressed as a percentage of the investment's value.

o Yield to maturity: The total return anticipated on a bond if held until it matures, taking into account its purchase price, coupon, and face value.

o Zero-coupon bond: A bond that does not pay interest during its life but instead pays a lump sum at maturity.

o This glossary includes some of the most important terms and concepts related to investing in stocks and bonds. As you read through the book, you can refer back to this glossary to help deepen your understanding of the material and clarify any unfamiliar terminology.

A comprehensive list of important investing terms and concepts

- o Asset Allocation: The process of dividing an investment portfolio among different asset classes (e.g., stocks, bonds, cash) in order to achieve a desired balance of risk and return.

- o Bond: A type of investment that represents a loan made by an investor to a borrower (usually a company or government). Bonds pay interest to the investor at a fixed rate, and the principal is typically repaid at a specified future date.

- o Broker: A person or company that facilitates the buying and selling of investments on behalf of investors.

- o Capital Gain: The profit earned when an investment is sold for more than its purchase price.

- o Dividend: A portion of a company's profits that is paid out to shareholders.

- o Diversification: The practice of investing in a variety of different assets in order to reduce risk.

- o Exchange-Traded Fund (ETF): An investment fund that is traded on a stock exchange and holds a basket of investments (e.g., stocks, bonds) that tracks an index.

- o Expense Ratio: The percentage of an investment's assets that are used to cover the fund's expenses (e.g., management fees).

- o Index Fund: A type of mutual fund that tracks the performance of a particular market index (e.g., the S&P 500).

- o Initial Public Offering (IPO): The process of a private company going public by selling shares of stock to the general public for the first time.

- o Interest Rate: The amount charged by a lender (e.g., a bank) for the use of borrowed money.

- o Market Capitalization: The total value of a company's outstanding shares of stock.

- o Mutual Fund: An investment fund that pools money from multiple investors to purchase a diversified portfolio of assets (e.g., stocks, bonds).

- o Price-to-Earnings Ratio (P/E Ratio): A measure of a company's stock price relative to its earnings.

- o Return on Investment (ROI): The profit or loss earned on an investment, expressed as a percentage of the initial investment.

- o Risk: The potential for an investment to lose value or not perform as expected.

- o Stock: A type of investment that represents ownership in a company. Stocks may pay dividends to shareholders and can be bought and sold on stock exchanges.

- o Stock Market: A market where stocks are bought and sold.

o   Tax-Advantaged Account: An investment account that offers tax benefits to investors, such as tax-deferred growth or tax-free withdrawals.

o   Volatility: A measure of the degree of variation in an investment's value over time.

Devon R. Blackwell

www.ingramcontent.com/pod-product-compliance
Lightning Source LLC
Chambersburg PA
CBHW070812220526
45466CB00002B/649